EPISODE 26

A Comedy in Two Acts

by
HOWARD KORDER

SAMUEL FRENCH, INC.
45 WEST 25TH STREET   NEW YORK 10010
7623 SUNSET BOULEVARD HOLLYWOOD 90046
LONDON   TORONTO

IMPORTANT BILLING AND CREDIT REQUIREMENTS

All producers of EPISODE 26 must give credit to the Author of the Play in all programs distributed in connection with performances of the Play and in all instances in which the title of the Play appears for purposes of advertising, publicizing or otherwise exploiting the Play and/or a production. The name of the Author must also appear on a separate line, in which no other name appears, immediately following the title, and must appear in size of type not less than fifty percent the size of the title type.

EPISODE 26 was first presented in New York City by the Lamb's Theater Company. The production was directed by Christopher Catt. The set was designed by Michael C. Smith. The lighting was by Heather Carson. Costumes were by Andrea N. Carini. Robert Mark Kalfin was the stage manager. The production opened on April 15, 1985, with the following cast:

Buzz Gatecrasher . . . . A.C. Weary

Hillen Dale. . . . . Diane Heles

Vaknor. . . . . Eric Booth

Dr. Arthur Deco. . . . . Jack Schmidt

Wallaneeba/Female Servant . . . . Marek Johnson

Contract Player #1 (Arno/Mr. Gatecrasher/
    Photographer/Guard) . . . . James W. Monitor

Contract Player #2 (Zugdish/Zargo Phildrooni/
    Voice of Komo). Daniel Wirth

Contract Player #3 (Garga/Wild-eyed Man/
    Worker) . . . . Dan Delafield

Contract Player #4 (Dave/Guard From the Lost
    Asteroid/Etherscope Operator/Scribe/Guard/
    Announcer . . . . Tom Flagg

CHARACTERS

BUZZ GATECRASHER, a young man
HILLEN DALE, his girl friend, a skilled aqua-ballerina
DR. ARTHUR DECO, a scientific genius, early 60's
VAKNOR, an Emperor of the Universe, ancient but well-
   preserved
ARNO, a King, heavy-set, with wings
WALLANEEBA, a savage woman
GARGA, a High Priest, sly and conniving
ZUGDISH, a Moro-Man, dim but mean
DAVE, a mechanical individual
MR. GATECRASHER, a prominent businessman
ZARGO PHILDROONI, a personal growth counselor
   (not human)
MAN, wild-eyed, with ray gun
GUARD FROM THE LOST ASTEROID
ETHERSCOPE OPERATOR
A FEMALE SERVANT
TWO PALACE GUARDS
WORKER
PHOTOGRAPHER
ANNOUNCER
KOMO, a god (voice only)
SCRIBE

EPISODE 26 is intended to be performed by a cast of nine
— two women and seven men.

The action takes place on and in the vicinity of the distant
planet Darvon.

A bare stage is preferable, with props and set pieces
brought on and off as necessary. Both should be kept to a
minimum. All music and sound effects should be pro-
duced vocally by the actors.

SETTING

A unit set suggesting various locations within a vast Art-Deco fortress, in a state of extreme disrepair and cluttered with junk.

EPISODE 26

ACT ONE

In the darkness, a tinny, off-speed fanfare.

ANNOUNCER. *(reading from script, removed from action)* Gigavolt Pictures, the Studio of Distinction, Presents...

HILLEN. *(v.o.)* Buzz! Buzz, what's going on?

BUZZ. *(v.o.)* This buggy will never get off the ground!

DECO. *(v.o.)* Fear not! We will soon be traveling beyond the stratosphere! *(sound of a rocket, humming like a huge electric razor, launching into space)*

ANNOUNCER. This is ... BUZZ GATECRASHER AND THE COSMIC RIDDLE! Episode 26: The Price of Power! *(The following synopsis passes at breakneck speed.)* WHAT HAS GONE BEFORE. As you may remember, through the startling principle of RADIUM MOTIVA-TION, scientific wizard DOCTOR ARTHUR DECO *(lights up on DECO)* succeeded in launching himself and his two young companions, galosh-fortune heir BUZZ GATECRASHER *(lights up on BUZZ)* and curvaceous aqua-ballerina HILLEN DALE, *(lights up on HILLEN)* far beyond the orbit of the Earth. From the sunny calm of Minnesota in May... *(The various characters enter as they speak.)*

7

MR. GATECRASHER. Son, as you go through life, remember these simple rules. Be honest, be friendly, be first. And always keep a dime in your pocket. *(He holds out a dime.)*

BUZZ. Dad, can I have a speedboat?

ANNOUNCER. To the very brink of the unknown!

DECO. It's true! By reversing the poles on the elemental oscillator, gravity ceases to exist! Now we can reach the stars!

HILLEN. I've always respected the Hebraic peoples!

ANNOUNCER. The purpose of their remarkable journey...

DECO. I have discovered a new heavenly body, called Planet X! It is heading toward our world at enormous speed, and is made entirely of gold and diamonds! We will save the Universe from this deadly peril, bring peace to mankind, and find a cure for all known diseases!

BUZZ. What's in it for me?

ANNOUNCER. But their brave mission soon goes awry...

DECO. The Vibro-Coils have melted. We are going to crash into Planet X!

BUZZ. Let me out of here!

HILLEN. Oh, Buzz, hold me tight!

ANNOUNCER. The three ethernauts crawl from the wreckage to find themselves on a new world!

BUZZ. *(picking up a stone)* These aren't diamonds! They're just rocks! What are you trying to pull here, Deco?

DECO. You know, I'm thinking this isn't the right planet.

HILLEN. Buzz, behind you!

BUZZ. Good Lord!

HILLEN. What is it?

BUZZ. It's some sort of gigantic ... *(sound of a large animal)* lizard!

HILLEN. Aieeee!

ANNOUNCER. But their trials have only just begun...

SOLDIER. Stay where you are. You are now prisoners of Vaknor, Lord of Darvon.

ANNOUNCER. Before the throne of the evil monarch...

VAKNOR. Your world shall crumble beneath my fist.

DECO. But why destroy the Earth?

VAKNOR. Why not?

ANNOUNCER. But Vaknor's schemes do not include Earth alone!

VAKNOR. *(to HILLEN)* How white you are!

BUZZ. Lay off her.

VAKNOR. Throw him to ... *(sound of another large animal)* the octaroons!

ANNOUNCER. In the nick of time, a narrow escape — and a new friend!

BUZZ. You saved our lives.

ARNO. We fight the same enemy. I am Arno, son of Belgar.

BUZZ. I am Buzz, son of Carl.

ARNO. We will be friends forever. *(They shake hands.)*

ANNOUNCER. A quiet interlude...

HILLEN. *(with cameo)* And this is my great-great-great-grandfather. He fought at Bunker Hill. Was your family in the Revolution?

BUZZ. Ah, no, they were busy.

HILLEN. Oh, Buzz, remember our walk behind the bleachers?

BUZZ. The bleachers ... right...

HILLEN. Just think, if we were back home, we'd be married now!

BUZZ. I guess we'd have to be...

ANNOUNCER. Suddenly, an astounding discovery!

DECO. These rocks are pure radium. I will build another motivator!

HILLEN. I love your wonderful holidays!

ANNOUNCER. And a desperate plan!

ARNO. Arno is true king of this world, and he will be avenged! Let us storm Vaknor's citadel!

ANNOUNCER. But there is treachery afoot...

HILLEN. Doctor Deco's gone!

ARNO. We are surrounded. Draw your swords!

BUZZ. Can't we just run away?

HILLEN. It's too late. We're trapped!

SOLDIER. Seize them! If they resist, cut them down where they stand!

ZUGDISH. Come, Earthwoman!

HILLEN. No — no — NOOOO! *(They freeze.)*

ANNOUNCER. Can this be the final destination of a star-crossed journey with Doom? Join our intrepid space-farers as they battle for the fate of the worlds — join us for adventure — join us for suspense — join us for Episode 26 of ... BUZZ GATECRASHER AND THE COSMIC RIDDLE! All contents copyright Gigavolt Pictures Incorporated.

(Lights up on the Throne Room of VAKNOR's citadel — a vast, decaying hall filled with junk. VAKNOR sits pensively upon the throne. A SCRIBE stands by his side with quill and notebook.)

VAKNOR. Meditation number...

SCRIBE. *(checking the book)* Seventy-eight, your Majesty.

VAKNOR. Number seventy-eight. "On the Futility of Existence." *(He pauses, composing his thoughts.)* The silent grinding of unseen wheels—

(A gong sounds. GARGA, High Priest of Komo, enters hurriedly and bows low before the throne.)

GARGA. Oh most gracious lord, I do beseech—

VAKNOR. Silence, Priest! *(to SCRIBE)* Where was I?

SCRIBE. "The silent grinding," your greatness.

VAKNOR. Yes.

> The silent grinding of unseen wheels
> By traitor Time to me reveals
> What fools we be to cling to life
> This pit of horror, this storm of strife
> 'Gainst bony tombs do frail hearts knock
> To measured pacings of death-knell's clock.
> Hear it calling to you now: tick-tock, tick-tock.

(to GARGA) What are you staring at?

GARGA. My lord?

VAKNOR. I suppose you could do better, hmmm?

GARGA. I said nothing, Mighty One, but wish to tell you—

VAKNOR. Bah! You are ignorant of Art. *(to the*

SCRIBE) What do you think?

SCRIBE. I could barely write for the trembling of my hands.

VAKNOR. A most perceptive youth.

GARGA. But of course I found it stunning, your iambicness.

VAKNOR. Hah, you say that now.

GARGA. What suppleness! What color! What ... warp and woof!

VAKNOR. Woof? It had woof?

GARGA. Oh, a great deal of woof, your assonance.

VAKNOR. I am blessed with some small gifts.

GARGA. My lord, I bear great tidings—

VAKNOR. Do stop bleating, Garga. *(to the SCRIBE)* Orders of the day.

SCRIBE. The runaway slaves, Majesty, await your verdict.

VAKNOR. Ah, yes. Let their fate serve as example to all who would contest my will. Rip the flesh from their bodies, then have them disemboweled and fed their own entrails!

SCRIBE. You sure?

VAKNOR. Why?

SCRIBE. The Pan-Galactic Commission on Organic Rights opposes the use of cruel or unusual—

VAKNOR. What business is it of theirs! ... All right. Have them slowly impaled on filth-covered spikes, as rats gnaw their feet!

SCRIBE. Interstellar Committee on Aid to Under-developed Planets condemns—

VAKNOR. Curse their meddling! ... Buried in hot coals,

till they beg for death?

SCRIBE. Iffy...

VAKNOR. Decapitation?

SCRIBE. Well, I don't *think*..

VAKNOR. Let's go with that then. *(as the SCRIBE exits)* And tell them they're getting off easy! *(to GARGA)* Well then, your news.

GARGA. The Earthpeople, sire, have been seen outside the castle—

VAKNOR. Buzz, buzz.

GARGA. The Hawkman Arno walks with them!

VAKNOR. Do you think my wits dulled with age? I have put that sparrow where he will not trouble me. As for the others, they are already within my grasp. My plans proceed apace.

GARGA. The will of Komo smiles upon you truly, your slyness.

VAKNOR. How pleasant.

GARGA. May this unworthy one inquire as to the nature of your enterprise, your monumentality?

VAKNOR. You may inquire as much as you like. *(pause)* Things ... fall apart, eh, Garga?

GARGA. Constantly, your perceptiveness.

VAKNOR. Chaos reigns supreme ... and the grave awaits us all.

GARGA. Such is Komo's way.

VAKNOR. But not mine. My works shall not fade.

GARGA. This is blasphemy.

VAKNOR. The subject is closed.

GARGA. But ... the Earthpeople — do you not fear the blond giant?

VAKNOR. Gatecrasher? He is not a giant. I am at least as tall as he is.

GARGA. No, your lengthiness, I am sure there is a difference of several inches.

VAKNOR. In stocking feet we are the same height! Do you doubt it, scum?

GARGA. No, no, certainly not, most high ... no doubt it was the angle of my vision that prevented my realizing the full extent of your ... extension ... which, as is plain for all to see, is quite, ah...

VAKNOR. Yes?

GARGA. Extensive?

ETHERSCOPE OPERATOR. *(offstage, clearly someone holding his fingers over his nose)* Lord Vaknor!

VAKNOR. *(referring to a blank television screen over his head)* What is it?

ETHERSCOPE OPERATOR. The prisoners have arrived in the outer chamber!

VAKNOR. Send them in.

ETHERSCOPE OPERATOR. I can't hear what you're saying.

VAKNOR. I said send them in!

ETHERSCOPE OPERATOR. Look, can you hear me? I can't hear you at all.

VAKNOR. SEND THEM IN!

ETHERSCOPE OPERATOR. This etherscope is completely on the fritz. I'm going to send them in, okay? You getting any of this?

(A gong sounds as ZUGDISH enters with HILLEN, BUZZ, and DECO in tow, their hands tied.)

DECO. Stop with the shoving, you hoodlum! I'm not a young man.

BUZZ. Cut the chin music, Deco. We're in enough hot water already thanks to your bright ideas.

DECO. Oh, it's easy to criticize.

HILLEN. Buzz, I'm scared!

BUZZ. Will you please stop screaming? It's so annoying.

ZUGDISH. You will be silent!

VAKNOR. Dr. Deco. The lovely Miss Dale. And the headstrong Gatecrasher. May I welcome you back to my humble palace.

BUZZ. When was the last time you vacuumed this dump?

VAKNOR. *(eyeing him)* Ah. And how fares the galosh business, my young friend?

BUZZ. What would you know about it?

VAKNOR. What indeed?

BUZZ. Where's Arno, you creep?

VAKNOR. Zugdish, hurt him. *(ZUGDISH does so.)* I find your manners grating. Doctor Deco.

DECO. Yes?

VAKNOR. Your discovery of the principles behind the radium motivator shows you to be a man of genius.

DECO. Well, I like to tinker.

VAKNOR. In my laboratories is a little bauble that has baffled the greatest scientists of this world. It is called ... the Jewel of the Black Hand. The name is not unfamiliar?

DECO. I've heard it mentioned.

VAKNOR. Good. Begin your work immediately. *(clap-*

ping his hands) Take him away.

(A GUARD enters and leads DECO off.)

DECO. *(as they exit)* Easy, easy, I have bad arches!

VAKNOR. Bring the Earthwoman before me. *(ZUG-DISH brings her forward.)* Ah. She walks in Beauty, like the Night...

ZUGDISH. Yellow-hair.

VAKNOR. Yes, my little pet. Yellow-hair. *(to HILLEN)* Do not speak. I have great plans for you.

HILLEN. Buzz...

BUZZ. Let's not go off the deep end, Hillen, shall we?

HILLEN. Get him away from me!

BUZZ. Okay, Jocko, how about backing off a bit.

VAKNOR. Zugdish, hurt him again. *(He does so. BUZZ collapses, rises to his feet, leaps at ZUGDISH. There is a brief tussle.)*

GARGA. He is very strong, the blond giant. *(VAKNOR glares at him.)* Well, no, not actually giant... *(BUZZ falls to the floor, senseless.)*

HILLEN. No!

VAKNOR. My apologies, Miss Dale. Garga, take her to my chambers. See that she is made comfortable. *(HILLEN and GARGA exit.)* Away from him, you brute!

ZUGDISH. Chow time!

VAKNOR. He is not for you ... yet. This pale barbarian must fret his role in our little farce to come. And then, when the final curtain covers all, you shall have meat aplenty. *(ZUGDISH gnaws on VAKNOR'S hand, growling happily, as VAKNOR gently strokes his hair.)*

*(Crossfade to a mine shaft in the Lost Asteroid. A group of chained
slaves shuffle by, holding pickaxes. Among them is ARNO.
He is stripped to the waist, revealing a pair of wings spring-
ing from his shoulder-blades. A GUARD stands watch.)*

GUARD. All right, you geeks, keep moving! Stop dragging those axes, you're making marks on the floor. Move
it, move it!

WORKER. My arms are weary. I cannot breathe!

GUARD. Spare me your problems, shorty. Lord Vaknor
isn't paying by the hour.

WORKER. He isn't paying at all... *(He collapses.)*

GUARD. Somebody pick him up. You, with the wings.
Let's go. *(ARNO does not move.)* Whatsamatter, you got
plasma between the ears? Pick him up! *(ARNO does not
move.)* Hey, butterball, get the lead out! *(He strikes ARNO.
ARNO wheels on him with pickaxe raised.)* A tough guy, huh?
What's your number?

ARNO. No one may strike Arno.

GUARD. Zat so? *(He strikes him again.)* How do you like
them apples, chubbo?

ARNO. You address a king!

GUARD. Yeah? Here's some special delivery! *(He strikes
him again. ARNO lunges at him. The GUARD pulls out his ray
gun and drops him in his track.)* Welcome to the Lost
Asteroid, jelly-belly.

(A horn sounds.)

GUARD. Okay, garbage, take five. No talking! *(He exits.)*

WORKER. You are brave, he who calls himself Arno.

ARNO. It did me little good.

WORKER. Because you are but one man.

ARNO. One man will do, when he is a king!

WORKER. There are no kings! Are not workers the true leaders of this world? Let us join hands, and break our chains!

ARNO. Your words are strange to me.

WORKER. *(handing him a pamphlet)* Then read this.

(The horn sounds.)

GUARD. That's it! Back to work.

WORKER. That was never five minutes!

GUARD. You want to argue?

WORKER. The Pan-Galactic Commission on Organic—

GUARD. Shove a bun in it! *(He strikes the WORKER.)*

WORKER. Help, help!

ARNO. Unhand him! *(He drives the axe into the GUARD'S back. He falls. ARNO and the WORKER exchange an amazed look.)*

WORKER. Comrade!

(Crossfade to DECO and DAVE, a beat-up looking robot.)

DAVE. Emperor of the Universe? You call that a job? Sitting up there, do this, do that, guy'd have a seizure if he had to button his own shirt. Think they'd ever put a robot in that position? Oh, no. Robots, they have no concept of responsibility. They don't understand money. They'd just blow it on motor oil. We all know that. I tell you, a little bit of flesh in this world makes all the difference. Here we are.

DECO. Where?

DAVE. Imperial Laboratory, Doc. Love it or don't.

DECO. Looks like a junkyard.

DAVE. Who cares, there aren't any *people* down here, are there. You want something, I'm around, ask for Dave.

DECO. Dave?

DAVE. Yeah, you'll recognize me, I'm the guy with the can instead of a body. *(under his breath)* Jerk-off.

DECO. Ah, Dave...

DAVE. Yah.

DECO. Maybe you'll show me where things are?

DAVE. Just like that, huh?

DECO. Eh?

DAVE. You could say please, you know.

DECO. I'm sorry, I—

DAVE. It's just a common courtesy. I know I'm not lucky enough to be able to sweat like a pig and lose my hair and have breath that smells like a rotting vegetable, not to mention all those *fluids,* gosh, I'd sure be happier then, but you might say please, you just might do that.

DECO. Could you please show me around, if it's not too much trouble?

DAVE. Why of course, I'd love to. How nice of you to ask. Over here is the Aquilia Memorial Magnetotron. The Magnetotron measures—

DECO. Memorial?

DAVE. Yeah, as in dead so they give a plaque. He had a little accident with the Jewel of the Black Hand. Good riddance to him. Over here is Lazripar Paradimensional Chamber. The Chamber allows—

DECO. Another memorial?

DAVE. Yeah. The Jewel again. Hasta luego for that chump. This here is the Krilvag Memorial Drinking Fountain.

DECO. I know ... he was working on the Jewel.

DAVE. Nah. Slipped and hit his head on a chair. But if you ask me, he did it on purpose. Anything else I can help you with? I'm only too eager.

DECO. Dave, I don't think I like this job.

DAVE. Join the club. Four years of college and this is how I wind up — Janitor in a Drum. *(placing a burlap bag in front of DECO)* Know what's in there?

DECO. I can't imagine. *(DAVE takes out an object not unlike a multi-colored bowling ball.)* So what's that? ... Please.

DAVE. Nothing, Doc. Just the Jewel of the Black Hand.

(Crossfade to VAKNOR'S chambers, where HILLEN waits uneasily.)

VAKNOR. Miss Dale. I trust you find your accomodations acceptable.

HILLEN. It's filthy. Look at this skirt!

VAKNOR.
    "A sweet disorder in the dress
    Kindles in clothes a wantoness." Eh?

HILLEN. What?

VAKNOR. You provoke the Muse within me, Miss Dale. Or may I call you ... Hillen?

HILLEN. You can call me Madame! Where's Buzz?

VAKNOR. Such spirit! Oh, Hillen, what songs you might inspire! I have got you —what is your phrase — under my chin. You marvel at my command of idiomatic English, yes? Obtained from monitoring of your radiophonic broadcasts. *(taking out a slim book)* A small volume of my verse. Will you accept it?

HILLEN. *(reading the jacket)* "Life is Hell."

VAKNOR. I make no claims to Art, but within those pages I have laid bare the essence of my soul.

HILLEN. Save it for Miss Lonelyhearts, buster. Touch me and you'll have the U.S. Government to answer to. My father's a senator.

VAKNOR. Listen to me, Hillen—

HILLEN. I want to see Buzz!

VAKNOR. Think not upon him! I offer you the riches of a thousand stars. You will be my bride!

HILLEN. What I cost, you can't afford.

VAKNOR. I'm good with figures. Name your price. Would you like precious stones? I will drown you in them. Gossamer gowns, spun from sheerest gold? Hundreds shall die in their making. Would you like to rule the world? There are several available. It pales quickly, but I would indulge you. Perhaps you are more practically minded? Yes. Universal T-bills with a six century deferment? Tax free solar bonds, looking very good these days. High-yield portfolios? Pharmaceuticals, strip mining, interstellar shipping? CD's, short and long term...

HILLEN. *(momentarily transfixed)* Long ... term...

VAKNOR. Yes. Very, very long. Oh, Hillen, will you not douse this aching heat within me!

HILLEN. *(snapping out of it)* I love Buzz, you fiend! Do you hear? Love — stronger than any bomb or bank-note you can name! *(She flings the book at him.)*

VAKNOR. *Love*, is it? Foolish wench, I will show you love as you have never known it! Come to me!

HILLEN. No.

VAKNOR. I will have you — now! *(He clutches at HILLEN, tearing her blouse. She slaps him and breaks away.)* You dare strike me?

(A SERVANT enters, hunched over and wrapped in a cloak.)

SERVANT. Maintenance.

VAKNOR. What do you want?

SERVANT. Empty the wastebaskets.

VAKNOR. *What* wastebaskets?

ETHERSCOPE. *(offstage)* Lord Vaknor! Lord Vaknor!

VAKNOR. Yes!

ETHERSCOPE. The Hawkman Arno has just escaped! He has overpowered his guards and is now heading fleenbix banocky!

VAKNOR. What?

ETHERSCOPE. I said he has overpowered his guard and clango yip yip fleenbix banocky!

VAKNOR. "Fleenbix?"

ETHERSCOPE. Beg pardon?

VAKNOR. Your message is garbled. Please repeat.

ETHERSCOPE. I'm sorry, the message is what?

VAKNOR. Garbled! The message is garbled!

ETHERSCOPE. What should I boil?

VAKNOR. I will deal with this myself. Over and out!

ETHERSCOPE. Excuse me?

VAKNOR. NOTHING! *(Pause. To HILLEN.)* How unfortunate that you cannot be persuaded. But the mind is like a piece of cloth. I can cut it to fit any shape. And I will — I will. *(to the SERVANT, who has been standing idly)* Don't work so hard. *(He exits. The SERVANT watches him go, then throws off the cloak. WALLANEEBA stands revealed — a wild-haired, Amazon-like woman in animal skins. Silently, she comes up behind HILLEN.)*

WALLANEEBA. So. This is his new toy.

HILLEN. *(startled)* Hello.

WALLANEEBA. Why, it even makes noises. Delightful.

HILLEN. Have you come to save me?

WALLANEEBA. I do not think so. *(With amazing rapidity she produces a knotted cord and twists it around HILLEN'S throat.)*

HILLEN. Guurcck!

(Quick crossfade to a prison cell filled with discarded packing crates, where BUZZ peers out through the bars. Against one wall, locked in chains, is ZARGO PHILDROONI, an insect-headed alien wearing a polyester leisure suit and an open-necked shirt.)

BUZZ. *(yelling out)* Hey, is anybody there? I wanna get out! Hel-loooo! Look, there's been some kind of mistake here, can somebody come by and open this up? I, ah, I'm sorry about what ever it is that I did, and I promise not to do it again, and I'd like to go home! Hello!

ZARGO. Don't apologize. It's weak.

BUZZ. What?

ZARGO. Apologizing's no good. It's a denial of responsibility. You've got to admit that whatever picture you're in, you painted it. That's the first step.

BUZZ. First step?

ZARGO. Towards changing your canvas.

BUZZ. Right.

ZARGO. I can show you how to do it.

BUZZ. *(ignoring him)* This is great. This is just *wonderful.* *(He punches the wall.)*

ZARGO. That's it! Let that anger out!

BUZZ. I think I broke my hand.

ZARGO. Would you like to share your experience with me?

BUZZ. Not really.

ZARGO. *(taking a card out of his jacket)* Here. My card. Something tells me you need it.

BUZZ. *(reading it)* "Zargo Phildronni, Personal Growth Counselor."

ZARGO. "The rich get richer, the poor get eaten!"

BUZZ. What?

ZARGO. My motto. I'm helping people become artists of their own lives.

BUZZ. How do you do.

ZARGO. I do very well. And so can you! You know the Lord Vaknor? One of the most powerful men in the galaxy. When he started my success seminar, I told him he was a weakling, a coward, and a fool.

BUZZ. What happened?

ZARGO. He threw me in jail for the rest of my life.

BUZZ. Too bad.

ZARGO. I consider it a tremendous breakthrough. What's your name, pilgrim?

BUZZ. Buzz. Buzz Gatecrasher.

ZARGO. How are you painting *your* canvas, Buzz?

BUZZ. Well, I'm sort of on this mission to, you know, save the universe.

ZARGO. And you find that fulfilling?

BUZZ. It's the right thing to do, isn't it? Good, evil, that whole thing?

ZARGO. Big words, Buzz. How do you *feel* about it?

BUZZ. Hey, I didn't ask for this. Some lunatic wants to destroy the human race, okay, it's bad. But I got problems of my own, you know?

ZARGO. Go on with that.

BUZZ. Not to mention that it's absolutely *ruining* my summer vacation. I would have been better off selling galoshes door to door.

ZARGO. Talk to me about galoshes, Buzz.

BUZZ. They're a kind of ... rubber shoe.

ZARGO. Are they?

BUZZ. Yeah. My father makes 'em.

ZARGO. Does he?

BUZZ. Yes! You ... put them *on* ... when it rains!

ZARGO. Why do you do that, Buzz? *(pause)* Buzz, as your growth counselor, there's something I have to tell you. I think you're a weakling, a coward and a fool.

BUZZ. Oh, shut up.

ZARGO. Hit a nerve, did I?

BUZZ. *(examining the floor)* Maybe I could dig a tunnel

out of here...

ZARGO. Why?

BUZZ. Why do you think? To escape!

ZARGO. Escape from what?

BUZZ. From here! From being trapped against my will!

ZARGO. Ah! But *is* it against your will? Or do you really *want* to be here?

BUZZ. What?

ZARGO. Buzz, *why are you running away from success?*

BUZZ. What's in these crates?

ZARGO. What do you *want* to be in the crates?

BUZZ. Be quiet. (*He begins rummaging through the crates.*) Look at all this junk ... cereal boxes ... candy wrappers ... doesn't Vaknor ever throw anything out? ... pillowcases ... lunch pails, for pete's sake ... and ... jeepers! (*He pulls out a small metal block.*)

ZARGO. What's that?

BUZZ. Looks like ... an injection mold...

ZARGO. Talk to me about injection molds, Buzz.

BUZZ. Well, you pour hot rubber in this hole here ... you wait a few minutes ... and then you've got yourself a nice new — galosh...

ZARGO. We're back on that again, are we?

(*Suddenly the lid of the crate behind BUZZ springs open, and a MAN, wild-eyed and disheveled, pops out, grabs him around the neck, and points a ray-gun at his head.*)

MAN. Don't move. I'll blow your head off if you move.

Buzz. Sure. No problem on the moving.

(Crossfade to VAKNOR'S chambers, where WALLANEEBA is still strangling HILLEN.)

WALLANEEBA. You thought to usurp me, eh? To cast me from my seat? You will not find it so easy!

HILLEN. Guurcck!

WALLANEEBA. There can be only one concubine to the Lord Vaknor — and that shall be — Wallaneeba!

HILLEN. Walla — gurrcck!

WALLANEEBA. Wallaneeba! She Who Lights the Stars! Now tell me — how would you like to die?

HILLEN. Of — old — age! *(She grabs WALLANEEBA'S wrists and flips her over.)*

WALLANEEBA. *(Drops the cord and lands on her feet.)* You wish to fight, do you? Good! But know this, worm — in me the blood of the warrior queens of Benzocaine runs pure!

HILLEN. Queens of Who?

WALLANEEBA. Let the battle begin! *(She pulls out dagger and leaps at HILLEN. HILLEN throws a pillow at her. She knocks it aside.)* You will have to do better than that!

HILLEN. I think there's a little misunderstanding here—

WALLANEEBA. Why not shout it from the battlements? Tell all the world — Wallaneeba has been replaced! *(She jumps on HILLEN. They struggle.)*

HILLEN. Please — let me explain — I don't want to—

WALLANEEBA. Spare me your lies, temptress! *(She lunges*

*at HILLEN. HILLEN ducks, comes up, and more or less acciden-
tally manages to plant a solid, roundhouse punch. WAL-
LANEEBA collapses, dropping the blade.)*

HILLEN. *(kneeling to help her)* I'm sorry — I didn't mean
to—

WALLANEEBA. *(Leaps up and grabs her in a headlock.)* Sentimental child! What a fool you are!

HILLEN. Please — don't — guurcck!

WALLANEEBA. Now let me hear you beg!

HILLEN. Oh, Buzz, Buzz, where are you?

WALLANEEBA. Who do you speak to?

HILLEN. The — man — I love — Buzz Gatecrasher!

WALLANEEBA. The blond giant?

(VAKNOR enters.)

VAKNOR. Well, Earthwoman, have you decided to —
(seeing WALLANEEBA) oh no.

WALLANEEBA. Adulterous dog! *(She throws HILLEN
down and charges at him.)*

VAKNOR. GUARDS!

WALLANEEBA. Let them claim your body!

VAKNOR. Away, vile woman!

(Two GUARDS rush in and pounce on VAKNOR.)

VAKNOR. Seize *her!* *(They pull her off and hold her.)*

WALLANEEBA. So this is what becomes of all your
promises!

VAKNOR. Vicious hellhound, I promised you nothing!
(WALLANEEBA breaks away from the GUARDS and starts

choking VAKNOR. The GUARDS grab her again.)

GUARD 1. Whoa, sorry, your majesty. She's a wiry one.

WALLANEEBA. Would that I had died a slave, than to have ever felt your sickening grip!

VAKNOR. Your love for me is touching.

WALLANEEBA. I long for your death, and well you know it.

VAKNOR. Then you have no grounds for complaint. *(She breaks away again and atacks him. The GUARDS pull her off.)*

GUARD 2. Scuse me, your majesty. My hand got a cramp.

VAKNOR. The punishment!

GUARDS. My lord!

VAKNOR. Her eyes.

WALLANEEBA. What?

VAKNOR. The Ray of Darkness!

WALLANEEBA. No!

VAKNOR. Then cast her out to wander the cliffs in blindness, till she falls to her doom! Take her away! *(WALLANEEBA runs at him and sinks her teeth into his arm. He bellows in pain. The GUARDS grab her.)*

GUARD 1. My fault, your majesty. Just wasn't paying attention.

VAKNOR. GET RID OF HER!

WALLANEEBA. *(as the GUARDS drag her out)* Beware, Vaknor, beware a blade in the dark! And you, she-lizard! You have not heard the last of Wallaneeba! *(The exit.)*

VAKNOR. *(Silence. Turns to HILLEN.)* You are probably wondering what that was all about.

HILLEN. It's perfectly clear.

VAKNOR. That woman labors under the delusion that I have paid her certain ... attentions...

GUARD 1. *(offstage)* Tighten the straps!

VAKNOR. ... Of course she is quite mistaken ... actually she is nothing more than a common slave girl with a vivid imagination...

GUARD 1. *(off)* Activate the Ray of Darkness!

(Sound of something like a soft-ice-cream machine switching on.)

VAKNOR. ... Very sad, really, but an emperor must show ... firmness...

WALLANEEBA. *(off)* The Pan-Galactic Commission on Organic—

GUARD 1. *(off)* Fire!

(Sound of a crackling electric discharge.)

WALLANEEBA. *(Off. She screams.)* My eyes — I cannot see!

VAKNOR. Although I will admit to a penchant for the grotesque. But why dwell on unpleasantness. May I ask if you have had a change of heart? *(HILLEN opens her mouth.)* Do not speak. A great happiness awaits you, Hillen, such as few women have ever known. GUARDS! Prepare ... the BRIDAL SHOWER!

HILLEN. NOOOO!

(Crossfade to the prison cell. BUZZ, ZARGO, WILD-EYED MAN.)

MAN. All, start talking! How'd you find me?

BUZZ. I didn't find — I mean I wasn't looking—

MAN. Oh yes. He'd like to see me served up on a platter, eh? He's not going to find it easy. I'll tell, won't I? I'll tell everything!

BUZZ. Tell what?

MAN. Don't ask questions, I'll blow your head off!

ZARGO. Talk to us about blowing people's heads off.

MAN. I'm sick of your drivel! *(He fires at ZARGO with his eyes shut. ZARGO collapses. The MAN releases BUZZ and falls to the ground, sobbing.)* I didn't want to do that! He made me ... I had to ... I had to...

BUZZ. It's all right. You just grazed him.

MAN. What? You mean ... I didn't blow his head off? Damn! I'm a complete washout as a traitor. *(BUZZ moves for the gun. The MAN snatches it up.)* Don't move, or I'll blow *your* head off! I'm not afraid to kill. You'll never get me in prison!

BUZZ. You're in prison now!

MAN. What?

BUZZ. This! Right here! This is prison!

MAN. *(pause)* Boy, am I *stupid!* *(kicking a crate)* These things were supposed to be loaded on the ships.

BUZZ. Ships? What ships?

MAN. The *cargo* ships, you fool! Thousands of them! What do you think he's going to put in them, eh? What do you think?

BUZZ. I don't know. What?

MAN. I'm not telling! Nobody horns in on my deal. Thinks he's got it all sewn up, does he? But I'll get there first. And then his Operation Spinoff will blow up right in his face! BAM! BAM!

BUZZ. Operation Spinoff? What's that?

MAN. It's supply and demand, isn't it? Whatever the market will bear! But you've got to know the *territory*. Once you know the territory you can sell them any— AAAAAAAAAAARRRRRRRGGGGGGHH! *(He slumps over, a dagger in his back.)*

(Enter VAKNOR, GUARD, and PHOTOGRAPHER with flash camera.)

VAKNOR. Well aimed, captain. You may remove the corpse.

PHOTOGRAPHER. A quick shot, your majesty?

VAKNOR. Certainly. *(He poses with the GUARD as the PHOTOGRAPHER snaps a picture.)*

PHOTOGRAPHER. Bee-you-tee-ful. *(The GUARD drags the body off.)*

VAKNOR. Greetings, young friend. I hope that gentleman did not bore you with his ravings?

BUZZ. It was just getting interesting.

VAKNOR. And what did you discuss?

BUZZ. Aren't you dying to find out?

VAKNOR. No. But you might be.

BUZZ. That's good. Who writes your material?

VAKNOR. Do not mock me, Earthman. Killing you would mean less to me than squashing an insect.

PHOTOGRAPHER. And give us just a teensy smile there, your maj. *(He snaps a picture.)*

(ZUGDISH enters.)

VAKNOR. You know, Gatecrasher, we have more in common than you might suppose. Mine is a tedious life with obligations to meet and bills to pay. Not unlike your own father, I imagine?

BUZZ. My father doesn't murder and enslave people.

VAKNOR. The labor situation here is somewhat more relaxed. Now there is a little project of mine for which an industrious lad such as you might prove suitable. As a ... representative, so to speak, of the firm. Agree to this, an I will spare your life. And see thet you get, shall we say, your slice of the tie?

BUZZ. How big a slice?

VAKNOR. We can discuss that later.

BUZZ. I don't do business with crooks.

VAKNOR. Ah, we find our principles in adversity. But perhaps I can persuade you? *(He produces a rubbery object.)*

BUZZ. ˙Hillen's bathing cap! If you've done anything to her I'll—

VAKNOR. You will do nothing! This she gave me as a token of ... her affection.

BUZZ. So? No skin off my teeth.

VAKNOR. In fact, the dear girl has vowed me her love...

BUZZ. But she told me...

VAKNOR. ... And soon shall be my bride!

BUZZ. That's a lie!

VAKNOR. Can you be sure?

PHOTOGRAPHER. *(snapping a picture)* Suck those cheeks

in! *(BUZZ, enraged, leaps at VAKNOR. They struggle.)* **Come on, people, let's make it fun!** *(ZUGDISH subdues BUZZ and holds him still.)*

VAKNOR. A trifle jealous, aren't we?

PHOTOGRAPHER. Sign this release, fella.

BUZZ. What?

PHOTOGRAPHER. Fabulous Faces Magazine. Feature spread on the Emp. "Galaxy's Most Lovable Dictator," etcetra. Come on, I got a deadline. *(ZUGDISH prods BUZZ to sign.)* All yours, big guy.

VAKNOR. You may aid me yet, Earthman. I will take advantage of this opportunity to further my studies in primitive anatomies. Take him to ... the DISSECTION ROOM! (He strikes a melodramatic pose. The PHOTO-GRAPHER takes a picture.)

BUZZ. *(as ZUGDISH drags him off)* You'll pay for this, Vaknor — my pop's head of the Kiwanis Club!

VAKNOR. How was that? Not too big?

PHOTOGRAPHER. Nah, the supermarket set loves this stuff!

(Crossfade to the Imperial Laboratory, where DECO tinkers with the Jewel. DAVE stands beside him.)

DAVE. Mind you, I'm not staying *here* forever. I got plans. For instance—

DECO. Hand me the protonic manipulators.

DAVE. Yeah yeah. For instance, there are lots of lonely creatures in this universe, they're far from home, maybe they just want to *be* with someone—

DECO. I need the klystron inhibitor.

DAVE. So I'm gonna start an escort service. Strictly mechanical, no skin types. Latest models, heavy-duty components, a few lube racks in the back in case they want to get private. What do you think?

DECO. Give me that green thing.

DAVE. All right, so I have to work out the details...

DECO. *(stepping away from the jewel)* It's done.

DAVE. Looking good, Doc.

DECO. When I turn this switch, ten million volts of pure radium energy will flow through this Jewel.

DAVE. What happens then?

DECO. I ... don't know.

DAVE. Could you wait til I'm out of the room?

DECO. We're finished for tonight.

DAVE. Great. *(He starts to exit.)*

DECO. Dave, let me ask you a question.

DAVE. Right now?

DECO. *(holding a crumbled sheet of paper)* I was going through some old notes I found, and I was wondering ... do you know anything about a Cosmic Riddle?

DAVE. Cosmic ... Riddle?

DECO. Yes.

DAVE. No. Absolutely not. I have no idea what you're talking about. I'm a total blank on that, I don't know why you're even asking me, I only work here! *(He exits hurriedly.)*

DECO. Dave, come back, I—

(VAKNOR enters.)

VAKNOR. Not leaving, are we?

DECO. Vaknor ... you're up late...

VAKNOR. Heavy lies the head that wears the crown, Doctor.

DECO. What can I do for you?

VAKNOR. *(producing a wine bottle and two glasses)* You can join me in a civilized drink. Will you? One of my more distinguished vintages, with a long history behind it. Your glass ... to the purity of science.

DECO. L'chaim. *(They drink.)*

VAKNOR. The ripe textures of maturity. Age is the great improver, wouldn't you say, Doctor?

DECO. It hasn't done wonders for my prostate.

VAKNOR. How old do you imagine me to be?

DECO. I'll say a comfortable fifty? *(VAKNOR laughs wildly.)* What, that's funny?

VAKNOR. *(Stops abruptly and flings his glass against the wall.)* Observe. *(He rips open his tunic to reveal a mass of livid scars on his chest.)* Yes, Doctor. You see before you a triumph of the embalmer's art. When your race was still grunting in the mud, I had already grown mighty. But my longevity has exacted a dear price. And my time now is very short indeed.

DECO. You're ... dying?

VAKNOR. I died long ago, as you would understand it. What I face now... Bah, enough! Within this Jewel lies the living spark of the immortal god Komo. Or so the legends say. And he who possesses it's secret will be ... unto a god himself.

DECO. Such an attitude!

VAKNOR. I want results, Doctor. And I want them tonight.

DECO. Look, I don't know enough yet — maybe a couple more days—

(DAVE enters.)

DAVE. Doc, listen, as one working stiff to another, about that Cosmic Riddle thing, I wasn't being straight with— *(He sees VAKNOR.)* Oops.

VAKNOR. On your knees, slave! ... Keeping secrets, Doctor? Very foolish. You will complete your tests as soon as possible and report to me — if you are able to. *(to DAVE)* What are you?

DAVE. Just Dave, your bossness.

VAKNOR. *(opening a panel on DAVE'S back)* You seem to know much, Dave.

DAVE. Nah, not me, your employership.

VAKNOR. *(inserting his hands)* You spoke of the Cosmic Riddle.

DAVE. Did I? Slip of the tongue...

VAKNOR. Or something more?

DAVE. No, no, I swear, I — I — get your hands outta there! I don't have to take this, I got my pride! You — get away — you think you're so important cause you got a little hair on your arms, let me tell you something, when the revolution comes, you're the first to go. See who's laughing then, flesh head! And the little guys, they're gonna ... and the big guys ... they ... you, ah ... and, um...

VAKNOR. Yes?

DAVE. I really like working here and I hope you'll let me stay on?

VAKNOR. You're terminated.

DAVE. Run, Doc! Get outta here before it's— *(VAK-NOR rips a mass of wires from DAVE'S body.)*

DAVE. *(spinning around wildly)* Malfunction ... malfunction... *(Mechanical components spring from him. He slumps against a wall.)*

VAKNOR. May your test prove successful, Doctor ... for both our sakes. Now, if you will excuse me, I am wanted in the surgery. I believe you know the patient. A young man named Gatecrasher. He is not expected to live. *(He exits.)*

DAVE. Doc...

DECO. Dave? Are you—

DAVE. *(as his parts drop)* I'm gone, Doc. He got my drive train. Just listen to me. There's this trash compactor down on six. Cute little number. Tell her I'm sorry but I ... won't be ... able to ... see her annnyymoooorrrr... *(He collapses, knocking against the switch connected to the Jewel. It suddenly glows from within.)*

VOICE. Who ... dares ... awaken ... me?

(Crossfade to ARNO. He addresses a large, unseen crowd. The WORKER stands by him, interpreting in sign language.)

ARNO. Slaves of Vaknor, hear me! I am Arno, King of Hawkpeople! Once Arno soared, high above clouds! He swooped and hunted, and ruled Hawkpeople in peace! Now Arno is chained! In dark caves he sweats, with no food, no water! He is prisoner of Vaknor the accursed! But Arno's spirit is not broken! He will break his chains! And he says unto you: Follow! Cast off your bonds!

Defeat the Oppressor! Seize the means of production! In the free air, as brothers, we shall soar again! *(The crowd roars approvingly.)* And now upward, brave rebels, upward to the ships! *(He rushes off to cheering.)*

(Crossfade to The Dissection Room. VAKNOR holds a single lit candle.)

VAKNOR.
> The winding sheet's a cozy wrap
> That warms us for a lengthly nap
> A bed of earth is rich enough,
> We have no need of softer stuff;
> Our only house a darkling cramp,
> Without the light of any lamp.

(He lights a nearby candelabra.)

(Its glow reveals the SCRIBE standing by his side. BUZZ is strapped upside down to a tilted operating table in the center of the room.)

VAKNOR. That would be...?

SCRIBE. Number seventy-nine, my lord.

VAKNOR. Seventy-nine. My fecundity impresses even myself. Have it printed immediately. See that it gets the usual reviews. *(The SCRIBE bows and exits. BUZZ groans.)* Ah, the subject is responsive. Now we may begin.

BUZZ. My sinuses are killing me.

VAKNOR. Does the dust disturb you? The air filters are temporarily out of service.

BUZZ. Listen, Vaknor, about that offer of yours, I've

had some time to mull it over, and—

VAKNOR. That offer is no longer in effect. Very sorry. *(He produces a record and puts it on an ancient Victrola standing in a corner.)*

(The opening notes of Bach's "Toccata and Fugue" are heard.)

BUZZ. What's that?

VAKNOR. A composition by your J.S. Bach. I find it induces in me a mood of rather divine melancholy. Or do you prefer the sunnier harmonies of Mozart?

BUZZ. I'd prefer to wrap my hands around your neck.

VAKNOR. Experience has made you bitter.

BUZZ. Look who's talking.

VAKNOR. I am Emperor of the Universe. It gives me a certain perspective.

BUZZ. Give it a rest, Vaknor. You can't even run this two-bit banana planet, let alone destroy the Earth.

VAKNOR. I do not wish to destroy it.

BUZZ. You don't?

VAKNOR. I was annihilating star systems as a way of avoiding my emotions. My growth counselor helped me get past all that.

BUZZ. Then why are you doing this?

VAKNOR. Does the phrase "subsidary rights" mean anything to you?

BUZZ. No.

VAKNOR. You are doomed to die in ignorance.

BUZZ. What about Operation Spinoff?

VAKNOR. Yes? What about it?

Buzz. Your little secret's out, Vaknor. I know what you're up to!

Vaknor. Oh? And what am I up to?

Buzz. *(pause)* You're doing something with galoshes! *(VAKNOR chuckles indulgently.)* You're not doing something with galoshes? *(VAKNOR shakes his head.)* Was I close? *(VAKNOR claps his hands.)*

(ZUGDISH enters with a small, cloth-draped cart.)

Vaknor. *(Lifts the cloth, revealing a glittering array of surgical instruments.)* Have you ever seen a vivisection?

Buzz. No, and let's keep it that way.

Vaknor. For scientific reasons it is best that the subject remain conscious. As I understand it, the pain is excruciating.

Buzz. You mean you're going to skin me alive?

Vaknor. Oh, no. *(He hands ZUGDISH a buzzsaw.)* He is.

Zugdish. Chow time!

Vaknor. Pan-Galactic Commission be damned! Zugdish, tear him apart!

(The music swells. ZUGDISH advances, revving the saw. He lowers it. BUZZ screams as the lights blackout.)

Announcer. *(off)* To be continued!

END OF ACT ONE

ACT TWO

Lights up on the Dissection Room, several seconds before the end of Act One.

VAKNOR. Have you ever seen a vivisection?

BUZZ. No, and let's keep it that way.

VAKNOR. For scientific reasons it's best that the subject remain conscious. As I understand it, the pain is excruciating.

BUZZ. You mean you're going to skin me alive?

VAKNOR. Oh, no. *(He hands ZUGDISH a buzzsaw.)* He is.

ZUGDISH. Chow time!

VAKNOR. Zugdish, tear him a—

ETHERSCOPE. Lord Vaknor!

VAKNOR. What is it?

ETHERSCOPE. The sensoscope has picked up a fleet of unidentified ships heading toward Darvon! They seem to be — what?

VAKNOR. I said nothing.

ETHERSCOPE. You sure?

VAKNOR. Continue your report.

ETHERSCOPE. The ships seem to — what did you say?

VAKNOR. Nothing!

ETHERSCOPE. I'm getting someone else's call over this thing. You hear it?

VAKNOR. No.

ETHERSCOPE. It's clear as a bell on this end. Did you say something?

VAKNOR. Stay where you are. I will hear your report in person.

ETHERSCOPE. Look, why don't you come up here so I can tell you in person. Hello?

VAKNOR. And so we part, Gatecrasher. I am about to be married and you are about to die. Qué hoorah, hoorah. Zugdish, are your nails clean?

ZUGDISH. No.

VAKNOR. Good. *(He exits. ZUGDISH, revving up the saw, starts toward BUZZ.)*

BUZZ. What do you think you're doing?

ZUGDISH. Chow time!

BUZZ. You don't want to eat me!

ZUGDISH. Yes I do.

BUZZ. No you *don't.* You only think you do. Now, what do you really want? *(ZUGDISH lowers the saw as he mulls this over.)* Don't strain yourself. Just say whatever pops into your head.

ZUGDISH. Yellow-hair! Zugdish want Yellow-hair!

BUZZ. You mean Hillen?

ZUGDISH. She make Zugdish feel funny inside.

BUZZ. I see. Well, pal, you're in luck. She's a personal friend of mine. Let me out of here and I'll introduce you.

ZUGDISH. *(threateningly)* Hunnngh!

BUZZ. No, really, I happen to know she goes gaga for

the sloping forehead type. You got it made. Just get me off here. Come *on*, she's waiting! *(ZUGDISH breaks the straps and throws BUZZ off the table.)* Hey, easy with the merchandise, Romeo.

ZUGDISH. *(grabbing him)* Go, go, yellow-hair!

BUZZ. Hold on. Something's wrong.

ZUGDISH. Hunngh?

BUZZ. You're gonna meet her like that? Maybe you didn't hear but the caveman look went out with the wooly mammoth.

ZUGDISH. Is what Zugdish wear.

BUZZ. Well, it's too loud. You want to impress her, sure, but *quietly.*

ZUGDISH. I do?

BUZZ. Tell you what. Take my clothes. Please, I insist. We'll switch. Let me have that helmet. Here, this is all cotton, very comfortable. You can thank me later. *(They switch clothes. ZUGDISH retains his club.)* Wait, wait, what's this club business? You going on a buffalo hunt?

ZUGDISH. Nobody touch Zugdish club.

BUZZ. A little advice. This is just the kind of item that screams low class to a girl soon as you walk in the door. You don't *need* it. I'll hold onto it for you. Really, I don't mind. All right. You walk in, you see her, what are you gonna say?

ZUGDISH. Hunngh?

BUZZ. Your line, what's your line?

ZUGDISH. *(after a moment)* Get down on the floor!

BUZZ. No.

ZUGDISH. No?

BUZZ. Listen to me. First you make eye contact. Very

important. Then you say, "Say, kewpie doll, how about you and me making a little heaven on earth?" See? You don't come right out and say it. But it works like a charm and I'm talking from experience. Now you try. "Say, kewpie doll..."

ZUGDISH. Say kewpie doll—

BUZZ. Wait. Turn around. Pretend you're just coming in.

ZUGDISH. *(as he turns around)* Say kewpie doll—

BUZZ. Not yet! Turn around. Wait till I say. Okay. One ... two ... *(He raises the club.)* THREE! *(BUZZ shatters the club against ZUGDISH'S head. ZUGDISH calmly turns around.)* Ah ... sorry...

ZUGDISH. Say kewpie doll how about you and me making a little heaven on earth?

BUZZ. Good, that's good...

ZUGDISH. *(lunging at him)* Get down on the floor! *(BUZZ steps aside. ZUGDISH falls over like a plank.)*

BUZZ. Have a nice nap, beetle-brain!

(Crossfade to the Bridal Chamber. HILLEN is being dressed for the wedding by a female SERVANT. A box of candy by HILLEN'S side.)

SERVANT. So I tell her, Honey, don't go looking for a snack when you're hungry for a meal. It's crazy enough to *begin* with, why make *problems* for yourself. Am I right?

HILLEN. Yes. Of course.

SERVANT. Now you understand I'm the least prejudiced person in the universe. But they didn't even have the same number of chromosomes. Well, love conquers all, as they say. There you go, dear, all strapped in.

HILLEN. Love ... conquers all... *(She begins to cry.)*

SERVANT. Is something wrong?

HILLEN. No ... I'm just so ... happy...

SERVANT. Of course you are, dear. But you'll get over it. If you need me, I'm next door. *(She exits.)*

(A brief silence. Suddenly BUZZ rushes in, waving his ray gun.)

BUZZ. All right, Vaknor, lay one hand on her and you won't live to ... *(He sees HILLEN alone.)* regret it?

HILLEN. Buzz, you're alive!

BUZZ. Hillen! Are you—

HILLEN. Oh, yes! I'm so glad to *see* you! Did you come to save me?

BUZZ. Of *course* I — well, I mean, it's no big deal... just thought I'd pop my head in...

HILLEN. Buzz, Vaknor wants to marry me!

BUZZ. Marry you?

HILLEN. He wants me to be his queen!

BUZZ. He does?

HILLEN. It's going to be any minute now!

BUZZ. Oh. Well. That's, ah, that's wonderful. Really. I won't stand in the way.

HILLEN. What?

BUZZ. Course he told me... little hard to believe, but... what the hell, ha? Congratulations.

HILLEN. I don't want to marry him!

BUZZ. First piece of trash in a cape that walks by...

HILLEN. Is something the matter with you?

BUZZ. Well, this is kind of a surprise. I bust in here expecting to find you rotating on a skewer or something, and you're stuffing your face with caramels. Frankly, I'm a little ticked off.

HILLEN. Buzz, it's been absolutely horrible!

BUZZ. I'm sure it was, Hillen. I bet it was *really awful.* He probably made you try on *all sorts* of dresses.

HILLEN. That's not fair!

BUZZ. Oh, please forgive me, huh? I didn't see you fighting any giant reptiles, did I? You didn't get thrown in a dungeon, did you? Nobody tried to skin you alive and eat you, did they?

HILLEN. Well, no, but—

BUZZ. Then there's not much more to be said, is there? It's pretty damn clear who's putting a little *effort* into this relationship and who's not.

HILLEN. I love you, Buzz.

BUZZ. Come on, drop the baby face routine. Vaknor told me all about it.

HILLEN. Told you about what?

BUZZ. Everything. You, him, the bathing cap, the whole shebang.

HILLEN. I have no idea what you're talking about.

BUZZ. A quick poke behind the bleachers and then it's goodbye Buzz!

HILLEN. Oh, really? Just who poked who? You and your kewpie dolls! If I told my father—

BUZZ. Your father? That lush couldn't see past the bottom of a bottle unless it was for a bribe!

HILLEN. At least *he* never had to change his name.

BUZZ. What's that mean?

HILLEN. Why, not a thing, Mr. Buzz-kowski! *(in an all-purpose European accent)* I pledge allegience to ze flag—

BUZZ. How's your mom's morphine habit, Hillen?

HILLEN. You little — immigrant! *(She slaps him. He slaps her back. She socks him in the jaw.)*

BUZZ. Ow!

HILLEN. *(pause)* I suppose you're not going to save me?

BUZZ. Do you want me to save you?

HILLEN. You can do what you want!

BUZZ. Oh, I'm going to save you. But after this, zippo. If we make it back to Earth, I'm looking for new fish to fry. Catch my drift?

HILLEN. Loud and clear.

BUZZ. Good. Now I'm going to save you. And you know *how* I'm going to save you?

HILLEN. How?

BUZZ. I'm going to tie some sheets together so we can climb out that window!

HILLEN. It's six hundred feet straight down into the mouth of a volcano.

BUZZ. *(pause)* All right, so I won't do that.

HILLEN. Can I suggest something?

BUZZ. What?

HILLEN. This. *(She holds up a vial.)*

BUZZ. No. Absolutely not. Forget it.

HILLEN. Dr. Deco said to save it for an emergency.

BUZZ. This is not an emergency.

HILLEN. It's worth a try.

BUZZ. I am not putting anything that clown made in my mouth. It's like drinking drain cleaner. *(Pause. They look at each other.*) **Hand it over.** (*HILLEN removes several pills from the vial and hands them to BUZZ.*) **Read me the instructions.**

HILLEN. "The Deco Reverse Evolution Capsule. An All-Purpose Pharmaceutical Aid For Home and Professional Use. Visionary genius Dr. Arthur Deco, inventor of the radium motivator—"

BUZZ. You can skip that part.

HILLEN. "Instructions for use. Capsule contains fast-acting ingredients which cause subject to undergo temporary reversion to more primitive life forms. Take one capsule for every million years of retrogression desired. Do not exceed recommended dosage. Avoid operating heavy machinery."

BUZZ. Okay. Here's the deal. I'll devolve until I hit something small enough for you to sneak into the wedding. When no one's looking, I'll pop forward and put the kibosh on Vaknor's nuptial arrangements.

HILLEN. You're so clever.

BUZZ. Don't push me, Hillen. Here's looking at you. (*He swallows a tablet.*)

HILLEN. Feel anything?

BUZZ. Nope. (*He swallows another.*)

HILLEN. Anything?

BUZZ. Nope. (*He swallows another.*)

HILLEN. Maybe you should be careful with those...

BUZZ. Another brilliant discovery by the visionary Dr. Deco. (*He swallows a handful.*) Probably bought these at a candy store. Any more bright ideas?

HILLEN. You don't have to be sarcastic.

BUZZ. Maybe we could ask your fiance if he'd mind

opening the front door so we could WHAAAAAA-HOOOOOOORRRAAGGH!

HILLEN. What's wrong?

BUZZ. Feeling just a little YAAAAAAAAAAAAG! *(His body contorts into impossible positions as he starts devolving.)* Oh say can you see by the only way you'll get me into that rocket is to peel out for a long forward pass then I want you to take a walk behind the bleachers with me Hillen Dale we will march the dusty trail when are you gonna let me use the car dad will be home pretty soon and if he catches measles that's why you can't kiss her I'd rather die first girls are so what I bet you a million ga zillion dollars that you did so did not did so go ahead and tell me a story mommy the one about daisy daisy give me your answer do doo gaa gaaaawaaah! *(He continues to devolve, passing from a baby to a chimp, then through lemurs, treeshrews, small rodents, dinosaurs, amphibians, lungfish, worms, and sponges. Finally he rolls off into the shadows, screaming. Then a large, oily-looking lump of protoplasm plops onto the floor.)* See? I told you nothing would happen. *(HILLEN screams.)* All right, Hillen, put a lid on it.

HILLEN. Wha — what are you?

BUZZ. It's me, Buzz.

HILLEN. You're a horrible-looking lump of jelly!

BUZZ. There's no need to get insulting. I think I have gone a little too far back. It's only temporary. Let's get cracking.

HILLEN. But you don't have any arms or legs or even a head!

BUZZ. That's never stopped me before. Is there a suitcase around?

HILLEN. Over here.

BUZZ. Help me into it.

HILLEN. Won't Vaknor suspect something?

BUZZ. Just tell him I'm something you're taking along for the weekend. *(HILLEN starts packing BUZZ into the suitcase. Her SERVANT enters.)*

SERVANT. Hello, dear.

HILLEN. Oh, hello, I was, ah, just packing up a little slime mold for the honeymoon.

SERVANT. A little advice dear. If a man and a woman love each other enough, they don't need any slime mold. And I think you know what I mean.

HILLEN. Yes of course.

(A gong sounds three times.)

HILLEN. What's that?

SERVANT. The wedding gong. The ceremony's about to begin. We'd better get you ready.

(Crossfade to the Temple of Komo. GARGA stands upon the altar with arms upraised.)

GARGA. O Great Komo, O Most Sacred One, accept these humble offerings as tokens of our obsequiousness. Yea, though we are not fit even to brush the Teeth of Your Magnificence, we do fidget and mumble with all due desperation. Give us this day your Holy Lather. Lead us not into Greasiness, but deliver us from Lint. For thine is the scrubbing and the soaking and the buffing, on Wood as it is on Formica, wax without buildup, okay.

(The gong sounds. HILLEN and VAKNOR enter. Behind HILLEN is the SERVANT, dragging the suitcase containing BUZZ. VAKNOR is followed by ZUGDISH.)

GARGA. You may approach the altar. *(HILLEN and VAKNOR step forward.)*

VAKNOR. How ravishing you look, Hillen. Fit to eat the band. Soon we shall be linked for eternity in the eyes of Komo.

HILLEN. Your bushman mumbo-jumbo means nothing to me, Vaknor. I'm an Episcopalian!

VAKNOR. I love it when you talk dirty.

GARGA. Let the ceremony begin!

(The gong sounds again.)

GARGA. We are gathered here before the Highest Throne to join in the union of two souls, Lord Vaknor, Most Dreadful Master of the Unseen Empire, and Miss Hillen Dale, Earthwoman and ... *(consulting his notes)* ... aqua ballerina. In the Holy Book of Orgute, Komo instructs us, "Yea, and you shall join together those parts that are broken." What does Komo mean by this? Anyone? *(All eyes turn to HILLEN.)* It's really not that hard a question... Very well. Komo here advises us that marriage is both good and necessary. It is part of the great Komonic Plan. In the Scriptures of Warg, we may read, "Take thou the smallest part of the cushion fruit and divide it thrice." What is the meaning of this passage? Hmm? Yes? *(All eyes again on HILLEN.)*

HILLEN. Not to be selfish?

GARGA. No, that's completely wrong. You're not even paying attention. All right. Elsewhere in the same passage we read, "Do not stroke the mane of the nar-beest, lest thou suffer my peevishness." *(pause)* Well?

ZUGDISH. Start your day with a smile?

GARGA. I wasn't asking you! *(to HILLEN)* Go ahead.

HILLEN. I don't know.

GARGA. It's *incredibly easy.* You have five seconds to answer. One ... two ... three ... four—

VAKNOR. Master Garga.

GARGA. Yes, your majesty?

VAKNOR. I suggest we leave this part of the ceremony and proceed to the heart of the matter.

GARGA. Of course, your vividness. *(taking out a bracelet)* Behold the Bracelet of Yugrok. Since time immemorial it has been the symbol of union among the Darvonian peoples. Do you, Hillen Dale, accept it as a token of your bond with the Lord Vaknor?

(a loud grunt from the suitcase)

GARGA. What did you say?

HILLEN. I, um, said ... yes.

GARGA. It is good. Lord Vaknor, do you accept the offering of this token?

VAKNOR. I do.

GARGA. The gong of bonding will now sound. At its tenth stroke, I will shake the Duster of Komo, by which we honor the Holy Cleaner, to sanctify this joining of lives. Let sound the gong!

(The gong begins its stroke of ten.)

VAKNOR. Soon, Hillen, very soon ... yes.

(another grunt)

VAKNOR. You seem displeased.
HILLEN. No, no...
VAKNOR. *(grabbing her)* How beautiful you are!
HILLEN. Get away from me!

(The gong strikes eight. Another grunt.)

HILLEN. Oh, Buzz, help me!
VAKNOR. He cannot hear you. You are mine!
HILLEN. Buzz!

(The gong strikes nine. The suitcase begins to move.)

VAKNOR. What trickery is this?
HILLEN. Buzz, hurry!
GARGA. No talking during the gongs!
VAKNOR. What have you done, Earthwoman?

(BUZZ bursts from the suitcase, seemingly restored to his original form.)

GARGA. The blond giant!
HILLEN. Oh, Buzz, you've re-evolved! Save me! *(BUZZ smiles and leaps fromthe suitcase, landing on all fours.)*
BUZZ. Woof!

HILLEN. What?

BUZZ. *(somewhat surprised)* Woof!

HILLEN. Sic 'em, Buzz! *(He pounces at GARGA.)*

VAKNOR. *(holding HILLEN before him)* Come no closer!

BUZZ. Woof?

VAKNOR. How refreshing to see you express your true nature.

BUZZ. Grrrr.

VAKNOR. But I have no time to play fetch.

HILLEN. Buzz, behind you!

BUZZ. Rarf? *(ZUGDISH clubs BUZZ with his fist. BUZZ collapses.)*

HILLEN. No...

VAKNOR. Finish your job, Zugdish. *(ZUGDISH advances.)* WAIT! Since this Earthman has proven so persistant in body, let us trifle with the fabric of his mind. We may persuade him yet. GUARDS! Take him to ... the Pit of Dreams!

(A nearby explosion suddenly rocks the Temple.)

ETHERSCOPE. Lord Vaknor!

VAKNOR. Yes!

ETHERSCOPE. We are under attack, your majesty!

VAKNOR. From whom?

ETHERSCOPE. Escaped slaves from the Lost Asteroid, led by the Hawkman Arno. They have taken our outer defenses. Now they lay siege to the citadel gates!

VAKNOR. Send out the garrison, you fool! Activate the disintegrators and enforce the battlements!

ETHERSCOPE. I'm sorry, send out the what?

VAKNOR. Why don't you fix that infernal device?

ETHERSCOPE. Sorry, your majesty. I keep meaning to get around to it, but... I was sick for a while, I don't know what it was, some virus or something, anyway it laid me right out. Then my sister-in-law came to visit, I had to take her around, and— *(VAKNOR lifts a curtain to reveal the ETHERSCOPE OPERATOR with a clothespin on his nose.)* Oops.

VAKNOR. What is the meaning of this? Why are you not at your etherscope?

ETHERSCOPE OPERATOR. There isn't any etherscope, your majesty. I was making the whole thing up. You missed a payment last month and they repossessed it. I didn't know how to tell you and, ah ... well. *(pause)* Are you going to hurt me?

VAKNOR. I... I... shall — NO! *(He staggers backwards and doubles over in agony.)*

HILLEN. What is it?

VAKNOR. Too ... soon — *too soon!*

ETHERSCOPE OPERATOR. I can see you're a little upset...

VAKNOR. Hillen ... forgive me ... I...

HILLEN. *(She screams.)* He's aging ... right before our eyes ... like a *mummy!*

VAKNOR. Yes... terribly sorry... excuse me.... *(He breaks away and stumbles out.)*

ETHERSCOPE OPERATOR. *(follwing him)* I hope this won't go on my permanent record... *(He exits.)*

GARGA. *(following)* Perhaps the words of Komo may be of some solace...

HILLEN. *(going to BUZZ)* Buzz, wake up ... please ...

wake... (*ZUGDISH comes up behind her. She turns. ZUGDISH leers at her.*) Why are you looking at me that way?

ZUGDISH. Zugdish like you.

HILLEN. Well ... I like you too, Zugdish, why don't you help—

ZUGDISH. Zugdish want to touch you.

HILLEN. We can't always have what we want, now can we?

ZUGDISH. (*grabbing her*) Hey kewpie doll how about you and me making a little heaven on Earth?

HILLEN. What?

ZUGDISH. Get down on the floor!

(*Crossfade to BUZZ, alone. A thick mist covers the floor.*)

BUZZ. I feel like I just spent the night in a kennel. (*shouting up*) Hello! Anybody there? (*His voice echoes into silence.*) Can anybody hear me? I'm trapped down here! Can somebody please get me—

(*A low growl comes from the darkness.*)

BUZZ. —out?

(*another growl*)

BUZZ. Who's there?

(*Pause. Sound of a heavy iron door sliding open.*)

BUZZ. Oh no ... not again...

(A figure appears in the shadows.)

BUZZ. Please, I'm not up to any violence right now ... stay back, whoever you are ... just stay... *(A man, mid-forties, friendly-looking, in a cardigan and slacks, steps into the light, carrying a black leather case.)* ...DAD!

MR. GATECRASHER. Hello, son. Mind giving me a hand with this?

BUZZ. What — how — is it really you?

MR. GATECRASHER. Well, if it isn't, your mom's in for a shock. *(They look at each other. Pause. MR. GATECRASHER shows BUZZ a dime. BUZZ runs to him. They hug.)*

BUZZ. Gosh, Dad, am I glad to see you! There's this maniac, Vaknor, he—

MR. GATECRASHER. Hey, you know what's swell about this country of ours, son?

BUZZ. Huh? Ah, what, Dad?

MR. GATECRASHER. Miss Liberty doesn't care who you are or where you came from. All she asks for is a little honest sweat and a friendly smile. And that goes for everyone — be he white, be he black, be he non-human. You take Mr. Vaknor for example.

BUZZ. You know him?

MR. GATECRASHER. He's one of my most promising customers.

BUZZ. You're helping him? How could you?

MR. GATECRASHER. Well, Senator Dale was kind enough to do a little bending of the trade laws.

BUZZ. Vaknor's insane, Dad. You don't know what he's done to us. Kidnapping! Torture! Murder!

MR. GATECRASHER. Yes, I've heard all that.

BUZZ. You have?

MR. GATECRASHER. It's in all the papers back home. Radio, too. Seems like folks can't get enough of your hijinks. You're a hero, son.

BUZZ. A hero?

MR. GATECRASHER. Not only that, you're a household name. There's a good feeling in America and you're part of it. And right now — and you may not be aware of this — you're standing smack on top of a gold mine. Let me show you something. *(He turns the case around and opens it. The words "OPERATION SPINOFF — EYES ONLY" are stenciled on the side.)*

BUZZ. Operation Spinoff...

MR. GATECRASHER. Mr. Vaknor's a big one for code words. Here we go. *(He hands a small plastic doll to BUZZ.)*

BUZZ. This ... looks like me...

MR. GATECRASHER. Not bad for an injection mold, eh? See how it bends? Go ahead, give it a squeeze. *(BUZZ squeezes the doll.)*

DOLL. Don't worry, Hillen, I'll save you!

BUZZ. I never said that...

MR. GATECRASHER. Now Mr. V figures we can dump 90,000 units a week with the right promotion. But once we crack the egg it's anyone's guess. Look here. Hillen Dale Little Miss Swim Set with Project-O-Rama goggles. Just like being underwater. Try 'em on. *(He puts the goggles on BUZZ.)*

BUZZ. I can't see...

MR. GATECRASHER. We can fix that.

DOLL. Don't worry, Hillen, I'll save you!

MR. GATECRASHER. Look at this. Dr. Deco Junior Genius Chemistry Kit with Self-Lighting Radium Motivator.

BUZZ. OW!

MR. GATECRASHER. Careful, you'll get a shock. Escape from the Citadel Wrap-Around Playhouse. Vaknor Pillow-Cases, 3-D SnapLok Lunchpails—

BUZZ. It's caught on my hand—

DOLL. Don't worry, Hillen, I'll save you.

MR. GATECRASHER. *(heaping it all into BUZZ'S arms)* King Arno Big Bubbles, Gatecrasher Goofy Gum, six flavors, Pop-up books, trading cards, breakfast cereal, toothpaste, rub-on tattoos—

BUZZ. *(throwing the merchandise down)* STOP IT!

MR. GATECRASHER. Something wrong?

BUZZ. Dad, can't you see that Vaknor is evil?

MR. GATECRASHER. Let's not get lost in abstractions. Now if you'll tack your John Hancock on this... *(He produces a lengthly contract.)*

BUZZ. What—?

MR. GATECRASHER. Just a formality. You agree to support the product line with personal appearances. Hog fairs, roller rink openings, that sort of thing. Plenty of free chow and a chance to see the country.

BUZZ. I'm not signing that.

MR. GATECRASHER. Son, I didn't want to get into this, but financially speaking, our chops are broiled. The bottom's dropped straight out of galoshes. We've just got to grab a slice of this tie. Don't you trust me?

BUZZ. I'm not signing!

MR. GATECRASHER. If your grandfather were alive—

BUZZ. Aw, Dad—

MR. GATECRASHER. Your grandfather was a great man. He came to America with half a doughnut in his pocket. When he died he had a whole closet full of suits.

DOLL. Don't worry, Hillen, I'll—

MR. GATECRASHER. *(Steps on the doll's head and crushes it.)* Now, are you going to cooperate?

BUZZ. I'm going to stop Vaknor if it's the last thing I do.

MR. GATECRASHER. *(pause)* Then let me tell you a little story. *(He puts his arm around BUZZ.)* When I was younger — about your age — a man I didn't know came to me and said, "Son, I like the look on your keister. I've got a million dollars to burn and nothing to spend it on. Got any ideas?"

BUZZ. Dad, you're squeezing me kind of hard...

MR. GATECRASHER. I said, "Mister, I may not know much, but I know what people need. And what they need is a good, reliable galosh with no fuss about it." I could tell I had him hooked!

BUZZ. You're crushing me — can't breathe—

MR. GATECRASHER. As it turned out, though, he wasn't a millionaire. He was a hobo who wanted a cup of coffee. But it got me thinking. Who needed money? I had a *brain!* *(He throws BUZZ on the floor and begins choking him.)*

BUZZ. Help! Somebody ... help ... me...

(WALLANEEBA, now blinded, dirty and ragged, appears through a secret passage.)

WALLANEEBA. He is not your father. You must destroy him!

BUZZ. Who—?

WALLANEEBA. Fight back. Use this! *(She tosses a dagger in his general direction. BUZZ reaches for it. His father grabs it first. They roll with the blade between them.)*

MR. GATECRASHER. And so I started with a storefront not much bigger than a broomcloset. It wasn't much to look at, but boy was I proud! *(BUZZ manages to get on top and turn the blade towards his father.)*

WALLANEEBA. What has happened? The knife, use the knife!

BUZZ. I can't! He's my dad!

WALLANEEBA. He is *not!* It is merely an illusion!

BUZZ. Don't you think I know my own— *(With a mighty heave, Mr. GATECRASHER throws BUZZ off and springs up, transformed into a ghastly monster.)* Holy smokes!

MR. GATECRASHER. *(grabbing BUZZ)* And darn if I didn't make my expenses back in the very first month! *(Howling, BUZZ sticks the dagger in. MR. GATECRASHER barely flinches.)* I knew success was just a question of— *(BUZZ stabs him again. He staggers back.)* —positive thinking! *(BUZZ stabs him again, turning the blade.)* Hired ... two ... people to ... help me ... traveled ... all around ... New England ... I was always ... very ... well ... liked... *(He falls forward, dead. Silence.)*

BUZZ. Who are you?

WALLANEEBA. I am she who is called ... Wallaneeba.

BUZZ. Wallaneeba?

WALLANEEBA. She Who Lights the Stars.

BUZZ. I'm—

WALLANEEBA. You are the blond giant of legend. From

a golden land beyond the stars you come to free this world from the yoke of its oppressor. This age will call you its savior.

BUZZ. Well, you know, just trying to do what's right.

WALLANEEBA. It is a poor outcast's glory to hand you the warrior's sword. *(She hands him a sword.)* And this meager cloak, which may mask your radiance till the time is ripe. *(She hands him a cloak.)*

BUZZ. Thanks.

WALLANEEBA. Will you go, then, and purge the evil from this day? Will you take your rightful place among the mighty?

BUZZ. Yes, I will.

WALLANEEBA. Good. But first you must make an important choice.

BUZZ. What is it?

WALLANEEBA. Make love to me now, or die. *(She whips out a dagger and holds it to his throat.)*

BUZZ. I'd have to think about that...

WALLANEEBA. No thought! No words! Nothing! Take me now, if you are a man! Then go and tell her that no mere woman can best Wallaneeba. Let her keep that doddering lech — the hero shall be mine!

BUZZ. Who?

WALLANEEBA. The whining cur, Hillen Dale! Am I not stronger than she? Am I not more comely? Do I not cause your very frame to shake with desire?

BUZZ. Oh, yes, certainly...

WALLANEEBA. Then why do you hesitate?

BUZZ. I —

WALLANEEBA. Or do you love her?

BUZZ. Well, of course, *love's* a pretty strong word—

WALLANEEBA. Love is the refuge of fools and children. The panting of dogs! Let me hear you say it, hero. Talk to me of love. Tell me of your devotion as I cut your throat!

BUZZ. Listen—

WALLANEEBA. Say it!

BUZZ. I —

WALLANEEBA. *(pressing the knife)* Say it!

BUZZ. I love her! *(He shuts his eyes.)*

WALLANEEBA. *(Pause. She pushes him away.)* Go.

BUZZ. What?

WALLANEEBA. Rescue your Hillen Dale and leave this place. Before it is too late. *Love!* Fools and children!

(A series of explosions rock the chamber.)

BUZZ. What's going on out there?

WALLANEEBA. The end of the world.

BUZZ. We'd better get moving.

WALLANEEBA. Leave me here. This shall be my tomb. *(pause)* Think of me, hero.

BUZZ. I can't—

(another deafening explosion)

WALLANEEBA. *(savagely)* Go! Go and find her! Tell her... she has *won!*

BUZZ. You're one heck of a gal, Wallaneeba! *(He runs off. Explosions, battlecries.)*

(Crossfade to the Laboratories. DECO holds the Jewel protectively. VAKNOR, stooped and shrunken, looks all of his four thousand years.)

VAKNOR. Come, Doctor, do not be foolish. Give me the Jewel.

DECO. Go take a hike!

VAKNOR. I appeal to you as a man of science. Will you see your labor wasted? It lacks only my touch to complete the experiment. Let me hold the Jewel!

DECO. Not on your life. It's not right for one man to have so much power!

VAKNOR. Do not babble of right and wrong to me. The hour of my doom is at hand. Give me the Jewel!

DECO. Why don't you ask nicely?

VAKNOR. Do not taunt me, Doctor...

DECO. Why don't you get down on your knees and beg, you shaygotz!

VAKNOR. You have gone too far! *(He leaps feebly at DECO. They struggle weakly, two old men rolling on the floor. The Jewel slides from DECO'S hands. VAKNOR reaches for it. DECO pulls him back. They fall against a telephone-booth-like machine. VAKNOR forces DECO inside and bolts the door.)* Are you familiar with the operation of the Paradimensional Chamber?

DECO. No...

VAKNOR. Then let me show you ... how it works...

DECO. You can go to hell!

VAKNOR. Why, this is hell, Doctor. Nor am I out of it.

DECO. Vaknor—don't use the Jewel—it cannot be—

VAKNOR. The rest is silence!*(He releases a nearby switch. An electric hum builds to a shriek and DECO disappears with a flash. VAKNOR falls to his knees and crawls piteously toward the Jewel.)* Life ... life ... I ... must ... have ... life...

(Crossfade to the Tower Room. GARGA stands facing two palace guards.)

GARGA. Is this all of you? Where are the rest?

GUARD 1. I think everyone else is kind of dead.

GARGA. Very well. Attend my words. A light has gone from this world. Our beloved Emperor ... is no more.

GUARD 2. Lord Vaknor's dead?

GARGA. He has been steamed in the Presser of Eternity.

GUARD 1. *(pause)* Can we go now?

GUARD 2. We'd like to get out of here.

GARGA. Contain your grief. All is not lost. There is a flaming brand among us to blaze a holy path to victory.

GUARD 1. Yeah? Who?

GARGA. Me.

GUARD 1. Forget it! *(He runs off.)*

GUARD 2. *(hurrying after him)* Hey, wait up!

GARGA. Come back, you heathens! Have you so little faith? I am the chosen vessel of Komo! His Broom will guide us! Then shall Garga rule in the name of Cleanliness! The Emperor is dead! Long live—

(VAKNOR strides boldly into the room, miraculously rejuvenated. His black hair gleams brilliantly.)

VAKNOR. The Emperor!

GARGA. My ... lord ... you ... you are—

VAKNOR. I am myself again. Scribe!

GARGA. A miracle ... I prayed for your life...

VAKNOR. Your end will be swift. But I have no time for it now. Scribe!

GARGA. That gem — is it not the Black Jewel of Komo himself? Long have I desired to see it!

VAKNOR. Away, you wretch! Scribe! Scribe, come hither!

(BUZZ enters, cloaked.)

VAKNOR. Idiot! Did you not hear me call?

BUZZ. No. Ah, sorry.

VAKNOR. The etherscope is inoperative. Tell the fleet commander to launch the ships at once. Operation Spinoff is now underway. What are you waiting for? Go! *(BUZZ slowly turns.)* Hold! Come here. The madness is upon me. Take down these verses!

> Death, thou art a niggardly thing,
> Peasant rags, unfit for a king!
> With joyous hands I—

Why are you not writing?

BUZZ. Because it stinks.

VAKNOR. Impertinent whelp! Your insolence shall be ... come closer. You are not my scribe ... you are...

BUZZ. *(throwing off his cloak)* It ain't Joyce Kilmer! *(He draws his sword.)*

VAKNOR. You have quite outworn your welcome.

Buzz. Did you dye your hair?

Vaknor. Taste the power of a new god! *(He holds out the Jewel. It glows brightly.)*

Buzz. What's that?

Vaknor. A legacy of the late Dr. Deco.

Buzz. Dr. Deco dead?

Vaknor. Decidedly.

Buzz. Where's Hillen?

Vaknor. Beyond your reach. Goodbye, you tick. *(He points the Jewel at BUZZ. BUZZ'S sword flies from his hand. He recoils in pain.)*

(An explosion rocks the tower. Debris falls from the ceiling, knocking VAKNOR to the floor. The Jewel slips from his grip and rolls away. GARGA, cowering in the background, disappears under a pile of rubble. BUZZ leaps on VAKNOR and they struggle fiercely.)

Vaknor. You should have listened to me, Gatecrasher. We might have been partners.

Buzz. Your money stinks, Vaknor, and so do you!

Vaknor. Oh, how common. *(He beats BUZZ back with several powerful blows. BUZZ falls near his sword, picks it up, and swings it at VAKNOR, who tears it out of his grasp by the blade. He kicks BUZZ to the ground, and, bestriding him, lifts the sword for a killing stroke.)* You have no head for business.

(Suddenly WALLANEEBA runs on with a savage shriek and leaps onto VAKNOR'S back.)

Wallaneeba. *(raising her dagger)* Vengenance is mine!

(She drives the blade into his chest.)

VAKNOR. Infernal she-wolf! *(He throws her off and staggers back.)*

WALLANEEBA. The gods grant me sight, to watch you die!

VAKNOR. No, no ... not yet ... not... *(WALLANEEBA stabs him in the back with another dagger.)* NOOOOOOOO! You ... you ... will... *(He collapses and does not move.)*

WALLANEEBA. Is he dead?

BUZZ. I think so.

WALLANEEBA. Then I have nothing left to live for. *(She takes out yet another dagger and points it at her breast.)*

BUZZ. *(trying to restrain her)* You crazy—

WALLANEEBA. Let me die!

BUZZ. Pardon me... *(He knocks her out.)*

(ARNO enters.)

ARNO. Buzz? Buzz, my friend! This is inded a happy surprise!

BUZZ. Arno, you old canary! Is that your little party outside?

ARNO. Ha! Yes. But we still seek the guest of honor.

BUZZ. You can stop looking. Vaknor's finished.

ARNO. Then victory is ours!

BUZZ. Whoopee.

ARNO. Why are your spirits so low? This is a time to rejoice!

BUZZ. I've got nothing to be happy about.

ARNO. Do not tell me our friends— *(BUZZ looks away.)* Arno's heart lies heavy with this news.

BUZZ. At least you got what you wanted. Now you're king of Darvon.

ARNO. There are no kings, Buzz. Only workers marching side by side into the light of a new day.

BUZZ. What?

ARNO. *(handing BUZZ a pamphlet)* Read this.

BUZZ. "Marxism for Beginners"?

ARNO. That book changed Arno's life.

(DECO enters.)

DECO. Hey, Gatecrasher!

BUZZ. Deco? You're alive ... you're alive!

DECO. Well, not exactly. I'm kind of in the fifth dimension. Shalom, Arno, nice to see you. *(ARNO nods courteously.)*

BUZZ. How did—

DECO. Who knows. Vaknor turned some crazy beam on me. What a mishegos! Anyway, I'm in phase here for about six minutes, so I thought I'd drop by and see how things was going.

BUZZ. Hillen's gone, Deco. I've lost her.

DECO. Listen, it happens. I remember one summer on DeKalb Avenue—

BUZZ. But I loved her!

DECO. *(uneasily)* Life can be funny that way... *(He starts to exit.)*

BUZZ. Stay right there, Deco. This is all your fault. You made me come here. You and your idiotic schemes!

DECO. All right, so I made a mistake, what do you want?

BUZZ. I want to beat the crap out of you!

DECO. Language! *(BUZZ starts for him but finds himself unable to move. He looks down to see VAKNOR'S hands wrapped around his ankles.)*

BUZZ. What the—

VAKNOR. *(Pulls his feet out from under him and leaps up.)* I am risen!

BUZZ. You're dead!

VAKNOR. Yes and no.

ARNO. *(charging at VAKNOR)* Evil One, defend yourself!

VAKNOR. *(throwing him off)* Away, bird-boy! *(He yanks the blade out of his chest.)* Know you now that I cannot be killed. But, happily, you can! *(He tackles BUZZ.)*

(GARGA rises up from behind the debris, holding the Jewel aloft.)

GARGA. You will remain still!

VAKNOR. Garga, you fool! Put it down!

GARGA. No! You are blasphemers all! Repent or be squeezed through the Holy Wringer!

BUZZ. What's he talking about?

GARGA. I am the pourer of the Timeless Detergent. We must be washed! We must all be washed from this sinful earth, and hung to dry on the Line of Komo. Cycle me, Lord! Spin and rinse me! I come, I come!

(The Jewel emits a rising shriek.)

VAKNOR. No, Garga, you must not, you must—

(His words are lost in a tremendous roar. The voice of KOMO booms out from the Jewel.)

KOMO. Infidel! Your hour has come.

GARGA. The Voice of Komo! Praise be!

KOMO. Vaknor! I gave you life beyond your days. Now you will surrender your soul.

VAKNOR. So soon? I need more time!

KOMO. You had four thousand years.

VAKNOR. Yes, of course—

KOMO. You could have gotten up an hour earlier in the morning. Look at this place — it's a mess!

VAKNOR. I was just getting around to cleaning up—

KOMO. And you dress like a slob.

VAKNOR. Should I go change?

KOMO. Too late!

(A powerful wind begins to whip about the room as the nozzle of what seems to be a gigantic vacuum cleaner descends from above.)

GARGA. *(shouting above the wind)* It is ... the Heavenly Hoover!

VAKNOR. *(struggling against the suction)* Spare me, O Neat One! I beg you — let me crawl about — a little longer!

KOMO. Underachiever!

(The wind increases to hurricane force. VAKNOR is drawn up into the nozzle.)

VAKNOR. Ah, what an artist dies with me!

(With a wet pop, he disappears up the suction tube.)

GARGA. *(after a stunned moment)* The Tyrant is gone! I proclaim myself King! All hail Garga, Lord of Darvon!

KOMO. I hate you fundamentalist types!

(GARGA is sucked up the hose with a quick whoosh.)

BUZZ. *(silence)* Is this a good time to leave?

KOMO. Hear me, creatures that perish. I am Komo. Out of Chaos did I fashion the Universe. And what happens? Garbage everywhere you look. Nobody bothers to pick up a damn thing. There's free will for you. I'm going to destroy this universe and make a new one. A smaller one, with not so many corners for the dirt to pile up in.

BUZZ. Isn't that a little arbitrary?

KOMO. That's the way I like it!

BUZZ. Nice to be the boss.

(Rattle of thunder.)

KOMO. *(pause)* You amuse me, mortal. I will put you to the test. If you pass, you shall gain your heart's desire. If you fail, this universe and all within it are going straight down the tubes.

BUZZ. What do I have to do?

KOMO. You must solve the Cosmic Riddle.

BUZZ. This really takes the cake.

KOMO. In my long memory it has never been answered. Will you hear it, or should I just grind the whole thing into hamburger?

BUZZ. I've got nothing to lose. Go ahead!

KOMO. *(pause)* What is one foot long, black as pitch, walks on water, and never gets wet?

BUZZ. Ummm ... a galosh?

KOMO. *(pause)* Would you like to hear another one?

BUZZ. Maybe later. *(WALLANEEBA groans softly.)*

ARNO. *(Goes to her side.)* Are you injured? *(He helps her up.)*

KOMO. What is your desire? You have only to think it.

BUZZ. I wish to see—

(HILLEN appears.)

BUZZ. Hillen!

HILLEN. Hello, Buzz!

BUZZ. Hillen, there's something I've got to tell you. I love you. Let's get—

HILLEN. Dr. Deco, you're alive!

DECO. No, not really...

BUZZ. He's in the fifth dimension. Hillen, listen. I've been thinking. About you and me. I decided it's time we—

HILLEN. Oh, Buzz, there's someone I want you to meet. Darling, would you step in here?

(ZUGDISH enters in an ill-fitting suit and hat.)

HILLEN. Buzz, you know Zugdish, don't you? We just got married!

ZUGDISH. How's it hanging?

BUZZ. Married? How could you?

HILLEN. Just chemistry, I guess. He swept me right off my feet. Isn't that right, Zuggy?

ZUGDISH. Hunnggh. Yellow-hair.

BUZZ. But I love you!

HILLEN. That won't pay the phone bill, Buzz.

ZUGDISH. Hey kewpie doll, huh?

HILLEN. Zuggy, have you still got the sample case? *(He shows her the OPERATION SPINOFF case.)* Good! We'll hop the next ethership. When my father meets you, he'll flip. Maybe he can get you into politics! Of course, you'll have to change your name... *(They exit.)*

BUZZ. Hillen!

WALLANEEBA. I was not always as you see me now. Will you hear my story?

ARNO. Is it very long?

DECO. Well, that's it for this reality.

BUZZ. Deco, wait! How am I going to get out of here?

DECO. Oh, that's easy. All you do is — uh-oh, time's up. I'll have to get back to you— *(He disappears with a flash.)*

ARNO. Your tale moves Arno deeply. When workers govern, sexual exploitation will not exist.

WALLANEEBA. How kind you are. But you — my eyes! I can see again! Who are you?

BUZZ. It's me. The blond giant?

WALLANEEBA. You are much shorter than I imagined.

ARNO. Come. Together we will form an agrarian cooperative founded on dialectical principles.

WALLANEEBA. I think I love you, mysterious wingéd stranger!

ARNO. However, civil liberties may have to be suspended at first...

BUZZ. Arno, don't go!

ARNO. What troubles you?

BUZZ. I don't know, I thought... Everything's falling apart! You and Hillen and... Don't I get to... I did the right thing, didn't I? Wasn't it the right thing? I mean ... what am I supposed to do now?

ARNO. You are suffering from post-heroic depression. It will pass.

BUZZ. But I can't just sit here!

ARNO. Rest your heart. Arno sees past the sunset into the dawn. And he says to you: Have no fear. There will be a sequel!

BUZZ. A sequel?

ARNO. Yes. *(pointing out)* Here it comes now!

BUZZ. I don't want to *be* in a—

ARNO. Farewell, my friend! *(He and WALLANEEBA fly out the window.)*

(The ANNOUNCER enters.)

BUZZ. Arno, please, come back, I — What's going on here? Where is everybody? I'm the *hero,* aren't I? *I* stood up! *I* made a choice! *I* fought for what I believed in! I—

ANNOUNCER. *(reading from script)* Attention, moviegoers!

BUZZ. Who the hell—

ANNOUNCER. Gigavolt Pictures, the Hallmark of Quality, presents its latest epic of serial adventure in 39 chapters.

BUZZ. Excuse me—

ANNOUNCER. You cheered him as he battled strange beings on distant worlds — now join him as he claws his way from rags to riches right here on Earth.

BUZZ. Hey, can you hear—

ANNOUNCER. Be in this theater next week for Episode One of BUZZ GATECRASHER ... GALOSH SALESMAN! *(He exits.)*

(The lights close down on BUZZ.)

BUZZ. No. No, wait a minute, you can't push me around like I'm some piece of — all right, I'll do it. But I want two percent of the gross, not the net. I want residuals in perpetuity. I want a limo. I want my own dressing room. I want... I want... I WANT MY SLICE OF THE TIE!

(BLACKOUT)

END OF THE PLAY

AUTHOR'S NOTE

There are a lot of ways to produce this play, but as a rule of thumb I would say: keep it simple. Elaborate set pieces and technical stunts should be eschewed in favor of a certain inventive cheesiness. Like the various miracles in the film serials of the thirties, Vaknor's world and the things that happen in it should be less than convincing but somehow effective. The transformations, talking insects, and giant vacuum cleaners should be no better than they have to be. In the New York production, Michael Smith and Amy Darnton used a vast array of found junk from egg beaters to bottle caps to build atom smashers, ray guns, and the like, that were both impressive and ridiculous. Andrea Carini's costumes managed to convey character, period, and a sense of fun without overstating the case.

Which brings us to the live portion of our show. Pacing should be unnaturally brisk, sort of a *Front Page* in outer space. Actors should be economical in their approach, and, with the possible exceptions of Vaknor's Shakespearoid-posturings and the Tontoisms of Arno, avoid camping or "coarse acting" styles. As with the other aspects of the play, a light touch is all that's needed.

PROPERTY LIST

Cameo on chain (HILLEN)
3 wrist-ropes (BUZZ, HILLEN, DECO)
Club (ZUGDISH)
Bathing cap (VAKNOR)
4 megaphones (offstage sound effects)
Old notes (DECO)
Lab tools (DAVE)
2 swords
2 flower bouquets (wedding)
2 pickaxes (ARNO, WORKER)
"Marxism" pamphlet (ARNO)
Flash camera, release form (PHOTOGRAPHER)
Feather duster, bracelet, prayer book (GARGA-wedding)
2 ray guns
Business card (Zargo)
Injection mold
3 knives (2 rubber, 1 collapsible)
"Life is Hell" book (VAKNOR)
Knotted cord (WALLANEEBA)
Wine bottle, 2 glasses (VAKNOR)
Candy box, pill bottle (HILLEN)
Lizard tail (Devolution scene)
Gorilla arm (Devolution scene)
Protoplasmic blob (Devolution scene)
Victrola and records
"Operation Spinoff" case w/doll and toys (MR. GATECRASHER)
Suitcase (wedding)
Black Jewel
Script (Announcer)
Dissection cart w/chain saw and bloody instruments
Nightstick (rolled newspaper and black tape — GUARD FROM LOST ASTEROID)

COSTUMES

ANNOUNCER — White shirt, wide tie, pleated pants w/ suspenders, fedora

DECO — White shirt, pleated pants, cardigan, glasses; lab coat and goggles (laboratory)

HILLEN — Skirt, "bobby-soxer" shoes, letter sweater, blouse; wedding dress (Act 2)

BUZZ — Jodphurs, lace-up boots, letter sweater, shirt (later distressed)

ZUGDISH — Pants torn at knees, fur vest, wool cap; undersized suit (final scene)

VAKNOR — Tails, lace sleeves, cape (all distressed)

ARNO — Wings, head-dress, "gladiator" skirt, feathered armband

SCRIBE — Monk's cloak w/cowl

GARGA — Robe and head-dress

GUARDS — Jumpsuit, gloves, helmet

GUARD FROM LOST ASTEROID — Jumpsuit, short cape, hardhat

WORKER — Loincloth, wig w/long beard

WALLANEEBA — Hooded cloak (for entrance); fur-patch bikini top, short torn-leather skirt, legbands, bones in hair

ZARGO — Leisure suit, white shoes, roach-mask

WILD-EYED MAN — Lab coat w/"Market Research" stencil (distressed)

PHOTOGRAPHER — Jumpsuit, press card

SERVANT — Mini-dress, stockings, high-heel ankle boots, rhinestone glasses

ETHERSCOPE OPERATOR — Jumpsuit, unmarked baseball cap

MR. GATECRASHER — Pleated pants, cardigan, print shirt w/bowtie, fedora; monster mask (after transformation)

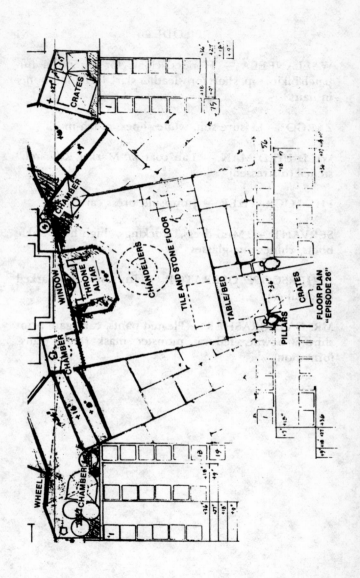

FLOOR PLAN
"EPISODE 26"

Other Publications for Your Interest

SEASCAPE WITH SHARKS AND DANCER
(LITTLE THEATRE—DRAMA)

By DON NIGRO

1 man, 1 woman—Interior

This is a fine new play by an author of great talent and promise. We are very glad to be introducing Mr. Nigro's work to a wide audience with *Seascape With Sharks and Dancer*, which comes directly from a sold-out, critically acclaimed production at the world-famous Oregon Shakespeare Festival. The play is set in a beach bungalow. The young man who lives there has pulled a lost young woman from the ocean. Soon, she finds herself trapped in his life and torn between her need to come to rest somewhere and her certainty that all human relationships turn eventually into nightmares. The struggle between his tolerant and gently ironic approach to life and her strategy of suspicion and attack becomes a kind of war about love and creation which neither can afford to lose. In other words, this is quite an offbeat, wonderful love story. We would like to point out that the play also contains a wealth of excellent *monologue* and *scene material*. (#21060)

(Slightly Restricted. Royalty, $50–$35.)

GOD'S SPIES
(COMEDY)

By DON NIGRO

1 man, 2 women—Interior

This is a truly hilarious send-up of "Christian" television programming by a talented new playwright of wit and imagination. We are "on the air" with one of those talk shows where people are interviewed about their religious conversions, offering testimonials of their faith up to God and the Moral Majority. The first person interview by stalwart Dale Clabby is Calvin Stringer, who discourses on devil worship in popular music. Next comes young Wendy Trumpy, who claims to have talked to God in a belfry. Her testimonial, though, is hardly what Dale expected . . . Published with *Crossing the Bar*. (#9643)

(Royalty, $15.)

CROSSING THE BAR
(COMEDY)

By DON NIGRO

1 man, 2 women—Interior

Two women sit in a funeral parlor with the corpse of a recently-deceased loved one, saying things like "Doesn't he look like himself", when the corpse sits up, asking for someone named Betty. Who is this Betty, they wonder? God certainly works in mysterious ways . . . Published with *God's Spies*. (#5935)

(Royalty, $15.)

Other Publications for Your Interest

A WEEKEND NEAR MADISON
(LITTLE THEATRE—COMIC DRAMA)
By KATHLEEN TOLAN

2 men, 3 women—Interior

This recent hit from the famed Actors Theatre of Louisville, a terrific ensemble play about male-female relationships in the 80's, was praised by *Newsweek* as "warm, vital, glowing . . . full of wise ironies and unsentimental hopes". The story concerns a weekend reunion of old college friends now in their early thirties. The occasion is the visit of Vanessa, the queen bee of the group, who is now the leader of a lesbian/feminist rock band. Vanessa arrives at the home of an old friend who is now a psychiatrist hand in hand with her naif-like lover, who also plays in the band. Also on hand are the psychiatrist's wife, a novelist suffering from writer's block; and his brother, who was once Vanessa's lover and who still loves her. In the course of the weekend, Vanessa reveals that she and her lover desperately want to have a child—and she tries to persuade her former male lover to father it, not understanding that he might have some feelings about the whole thing. *Time Magazine* heard "the unmistakable cry of an infant hit . . . Playwright Tolan's work radiates promise and achievement." (#25051)

(Royalty, $60–$40.)

PASTORALE
(LITTLE THEATRE—COMEDY)
By DEBORAH EISENBERG

3 men, 4 women—Interior
(plus 1 or 2 bit parts and 3 optional extras)

"Deborah Eisenberg is one of the freshest and funniest voices in some seasons."—Newsweek. Somewhere out in the country Melanie has rented a house and in the living room she, her friend Rachel who came for a weekend but forgets to leave, and their school friend Steve (all in their mid-20s) spend nearly a year meandering through a mental landscape including such concerns as phobias, friendship, work, sex, slovenliness and epistemology. Other people happen by: Steve's young girlfriend Celia, the virtuous and annoying Edie, a man who Melanie has picked up in a bar, and a couple who appear during an intense conversation and observe the sofa is on fire. The lives of the three friends inevitably proceed and eventually draw them, the better prepared perhaps by their months on the sofa, in separate directions. "The most original, funniest new comic voice to be heard in New York theater since Beth Henley's 'Crimes of the Heart.'"—N.Y. Times. "A very funny, stylish comedy."—The New Yorker. "Wacky charm and wayward wit."—New York Magazine. "Delightful."—N.Y. Post. "Uproarious . . . the play is a world unto itself, and it spins."—N.Y. Sunday Times. (#18016)

(Royalty, $50–$35.)

Other Publications for Your Interest

MAGIC TIME
(LITTLE THEATRE—COMEDY)

By JAMES SHERMAN

5 men, 3 women—Interior

Off Broadway audiences and the critics enjoyed and praised this engaging backstage comedy about a troupe of professional actors (non-Equity) preparing to give their last performance of the summer in *Hamlet*. Very cleverly the backstage relationships mirror the onstage ones. For instance, Larry Mandell (Laertes) very much resents the performance of David Singer (Hamlet), as he feels *he* should have had the role. Also, he is secretly in love with Laurie Black (Ophelia)—who is living with David. David, meanwhile, is holding a mirror up to nature, but not to himself—and Laurie is trying to get him to be honest with her about his feelings. There's also a Horatio who has a thriving career in TV commercials; a Polonius who gave up acting to have a family and teach high school, but who has decidedly second thoughts, and a Gertrude and Claudius who are married in *real* life. This engaging play is an absolute *must* for all non-Equity groups, such as colleges, community theatres, and non-Equity pros or semi-pros. "There is an artful innocence in 'Magic Time' . . . It is also delightful."—N.Y. Times. ". . . captivating little backstage comedy . . . it is entirely winning . . . boasts one of the most entertaining band of Shakespearean players I've run across."—N.Y. Daily News.   (#15028)

(Royalty, $50–$40.)

BADGERS
(LITTLE THEATRE—COMEDY)

By DONALD WOLLNER

6 men, 2 women—Interior, w/insert

"'Badgers! . . . opened the season at the Manhattan Punchline while Simon and Garfunkel were offering a concert in Central Park. In tandem, the two events were a kind of déjà vu for the 60's, when all things seemed possible, even revolution. As we watch 'Badgers' we can hear a subliminal 'Sounds of Silence'."—N.Y. Times. The time is 1967. The place is the University of Wisconsin during the Dow Chemical sit-in/riots. This cross-section of college campus life in that turbulent decade focuses on the effect of the events on the characters: "Wollner's amiable remembrance adds up to a sort of campus roll-call—here are radicalized kids from Eastern high schools, 'WASP' accountancy majors who didn't make Harvard or Penn. Most significant is the playwright's contention that none were touched lightly by those times . . . he has a strong sense of the canvas he's drawing on."—Soho Weekly News. If you loved *Moonchildren*, you're certain to love this "wry and gentle look at a troubled time" (Bergen Record).   (#3998)

(Royalty, $50–$40.)

Other Publications for Your Interest

COMING ATTRACTIONS
(ADVANCED GROUPS—COMEDY WITH MUSIC)

By TED TALLY, music by JACK FELDMAN, lyrics by BRUCE SUSSMAN and FELDMAN

5 men, 2 women—Unit Set

Lonnie Wayne Burke has the requisite viciousness to be a media celebrity—but he lacks vision. When we meet him, he is holding only four people hostage in a laundromat. There aren't any cops much less reporters around, because they're across town where some guy is holding 50 hostages. But, a talent agent named Manny sees possibilities in Lonnie Wayne. He devises a criminal persona for him by dressing him in a skeleton costume and sending him door-to-door, murdering people as ''The Hallowe'en Killer''. He is captured, and becomes an instant celebrity, performing on TV shows. When his fame starts to wane, he crashes the Miss America Pageant disguised as Miss Wyoming to kill Miss America on camera. However, he falls in love with her, and this eventually leads to his downfall. Lonnie ends up in the electric chair, and is fried ''live'' on prime-time TV as part of a jazzy production number! ''Fizzles with pixilated laughter.''—Time. ''I don't often burst into gales of laughter in the theatre; here, I found myself rocking with guffaws.''—New York Mag. ''Vastly entertaining.''—Newark Star-Ledger.

(Royalty, $50–$40.)

SORROWS OF STEPHEN
(ADVANCED GROUPS—COMEDY)

By PETER PARNELL

4 men, 5 women—Unit set

Stephen Hurt is a headstrong, impetuous young man—an irrepressible romantic—he's unable not to be in love. One of his models is Goethe's tragic hero, Werther, but as a contemporary New Yorker, he's adaptable. The end of an apparently undying love is followed by the birth of a grand new passion. And as he believes there's a literary precedent for all romantic possibilities justifying his choices—so with enthusiasm bordering on fickleness, he turns from Tolstoy, to Stendhal or Balzac. And Stephen's never discouraged—he can withstand rivers of rejection. (From the N.Y. Times.) And so his affairs—real and tentative—begin when his girl friend leaves him. He makes a romantic stab at a female cab driver, passes an assignation note to an unknown lady at the opera, flirts with an accessible waitress—and then has a tragic-with-comic-overtones, wild affair with his best friend's fiancée. ''Breezy and buoyant. A real romantic comedy, sophisticated and sentimental, with an ageless attitude toward the power of positive love.''—N.Y. Times.

(Slightly Restricted. Royalty, $50–$40, where available)

NEW OFF BROADWAY HITS
from
SAMUEL FRENCH, INC.

AMERICAN DAYS – AMIDST THE GLADIOLAS –
ARE YOU NOW OR HAVE YOU EVER BEEN –
THE ART OF DINING – BADGERS – THE BRIXTON
RECOVERY – CLOUD NINE – COLORED PEOPLE'S
TIME – COMING ATTRACTIONS – A COUPLA
WHITE CHICKS SITTING AROUND TALKING –
THE DEATH OF A MINER – THE DIVINERS –
THE FOX – GRACE – MAGIC TIME – MARLON
BRANDO SAT RIGHT HERE – MEETINGS –
MODIGLIANI – THE PENULTIMATE PROBLEM OF
SHERLOCK HOLMES – THE POTSDAM QUARTET –
THE PREVALENCE OF MRS. SEAL – PUT THEM
ALL TOGETHER – SAVE GRAND CENTRAL – SEA
MARKS – THE SLAB BOYS – SOLDIER'S PLAY –
SORROWS OF STEPHEN – THE SOUL OF THE
WHITE ANT – STEAL AWAY – STRANGE SNOW –
SUMMER – TABLE SETTINGS – TALKING WITH –
TRANSLATIONS – TRUE WEST – VIKINGS –
THE WOOLGATHERER – ZOOMAN AND THE SIGN

For descriptions of these plays, consult our Basic Catalogue of Plays